MW01173175

# INTERVENTION REAL?

---

TRUE STORIES FROM THE AUTHOR'S LIFE

---

Mervyn Byron

Phaelon Publishing

Book Layout: Spark by BookDesignTemplates.com
Cover Photo: Mervyn Byron

**Is Divine Intervention Real? / Mervyn Byron**

ISBN 978-1-7773097-4-9

Dedicated to all the people God has placed in my path that have given me joy, peace, love, and laughter, as well as anxiety, pain, and hardship. As all, were meant to teach me and help me to grow into maturity as I embraced the love, and also learned the patience I needed to deal with the difficult ones.

Even when I didn't do so well, it was still a learning experience that has helped form my current personality and allowed me to pass on to others the lessons I have learned.

You can either repeat the same mistakes or learn from them and grow more quickly in your relationship, without as much adversity as some of us have experienced.

---

You begin by serving your own needs.
You journey by serving the needs of others.
You end by serving the needs of the whole.
That's when the journey is complete.

—WALLACE HUEY

# CONTENTS

# Introduction

The following stories are firsthand accounts by the author. They are all personal experiences from his life and perspective, of what some might call miracles of *divine intervention*. These are not a compilation of sensational or embellished third- or fourth-hand accounts designed to be awe-inspiring, but examples of everyday encounters whereby *divine intervention* were present. It isn't an exhaustive review of all of his encounters, as some amazingly miraculous events were not included in this first book and may appear at a later time in another.

Hopefully, the reader will get a sense of what *divine intervention* is, and how it can manifest in so many different ways, either very small or of a grander design in the life of one person. Within this book, you will see that *divine intervention* will show up in the form of discernment and a warning of impending danger, confirmation of your path, protection from harm, guidance, and direction, calm in the face of danger, courage to act at all costs, roadblocks preventing serious mistakes, and providence exactly when it was needed. The goal is to help the reader recognize these events in their own life and understand their origin. Hopefully, that will lead to an attitude of gratefulness for all the love and care we do experience throughout this earthly journey, instead of those events just being written off as a fortunate coincidence.

Being open to the understanding and recognition of the influence of *divine intervention* may help to guide you through life's triumphs and struggles. But above all, one should be aware that a loving entity is watching out for our well-being, and we are never alone.

## Additional Material: Photo Gallery

Throughout this book, the stories you read will sometimes have photos to accompany the adventure.

These photographs are available for viewing at the publisher's website. And can be found there on the gallery page. (phaelonpublishing.ca)

We hope you will take the time to check them out and see that these experiences were real and taught the author to rely on the Divine help that was readily available to him.

# CHAPTER ONE

# Understanding

Before I get into the personal encounters I've had with *divine intervention*, I want to explain my thinking on the subject, and why I believe this way. I do not mean to say that anyone else must believe as I do. It is simply to offer a clarification for the reader, so they can be on the same page when it comes to an understanding of what *divine intervention* is and how one would access it.

## What Is 'Divine Intervention'?

The people, who believe *divine intervention* exists, already have the answer to that question settled in their minds. But to be clear, I'm not referring to simply receiving answers to your prayer requests, as believers will have a library full of those, although there are some stories here that relate to that aspect. I'm implying a sovereign act upon your life that you did not specifically ask for, but were guided into or through because it was to your benefit or the benefit of others in some way.

To those individuals who aren't sure what they believe in or don't believe at all, *what-it-is* then—becomes a big question! Each will base their belief on either their personal experience or what they have read about *divine intervention* from the opinions or lives of others, which may not necessarily mean it's correct or all-encompassing.

For those who believe it exists, they understand it to be an act of intervention by a supernatural entity. Some will *claim* it is an impersonal universal energy that surrounds us and reacts to our thoughts and our will. Others will believe it's a personal relationship and call that energy, God, or their Creator, Jesus or Lord. And claim that this Deity watches over us and that we can interact through prayer or meditation daily.

Others may say that *divine intervention* is the act of a guardian angel or spirit guide or an ancestor who has passed on and is intervening in our lives to try and help us through our human experience.

There are many other names used to indicate where *divine intervention* comes from, but I'm not here to tell you what designations to use. That's your personal choice, and there are better people than I who can guide you in that matter, but you do need a reference point and a realistic understanding of what it is.

The act of *divine intervention* may be interpreted differently by each individual based on their understanding of how it has interacted in their life. For some, their conclusion may be the result of having the wrong impression, because they have minimal experience with it, or thought their experience was negative. The only way to achieve a full understanding of what *divine intervention* is, however, would be to experience it yourself. Not just once or twice, but many times, and from different aspects so that a fuller understanding comes to light.

Since the interpretation is personal, and this book is about my own experiences with *divine intervention*. I refer to that source in my life as being from God. Does that mean it isn't a universal energy? Absolutely not, since my version of God would include a universal energy that permeates everything. Does that mean it doesn't involve guardian angels? Of course not, as angels are in the spiritual realm and are there to guide us on a personal basis. Hence, the term *spirit guide* is not out of place either. With that said, many people have a different understanding of what spirit is, and not all concepts might be correct. In fact, for those who believe in the spiritual realm, they would agree that there are definitely spirits with a highly negative influence in the lives of people, and their guidance is not for one's benefit. Unless, of course, you believe that there is no such thing as an evil influence in the world, in which case we have a difference of opinion on what reality actually is.

I believe that *divine intervention* is available to everyone, whenever needed, regardless of religious affiliation or belief. That's because I believe God loves all creation and is willing to intercede on any one's behalf. I will not use scripture to convince you, as you may not believe the writings in any sacred book, so that would be a waste of time. The best evidence I can present is to relay to you the many experiences I have had over my 63 years and allow you to decide for yourself if *divine intervention* is real. And of course, if it is, then you need to ask yourself some questions.

1. How many times have you experienced it and not realized it?
2. Why do skeptics claim it isn't real, and how much trust should you place in their opinion?

3. If it is real, how do you access *divine intervention* in your life?

I will try to address these questions throughout this book. The primary purpose of it is to describe the many ways that *divine intervention* has interacted in my life. To demonstrate that it can happen on a grand scale and also in the minuscule aspects of your life. The goal is to open your eyes to its presence in your own life and to give you hope. If God, the Universal Energy, the Creator, Jesus, the Lord, Guardian Angels, or Spirit Guides have interacted in the life of the author, under a myriad of circumstances, it will interact in your life as well!

## How Many Times Have You Experienced It, And Not Realized It?

Recognizing times of *divine intervention* requires a receptive mind. However, many may be so opposed to the concept that they're not able to recognize it when it occurs, so they conclude that it doesn't happen.

For those who do believe it exists, they may not think they can obtain it upon request, because they do not understand how to access it, and the personality from which it originates. Often those attempts seem to be in vain, and they give up on the notion that God would tangibly intervene on their behalf at all.

For those who do receive *divine intervention* but don't recognize it, for what it is, they often pass it off as pure luck, good fortune, or an accidental one-time encounter. But what if you asked for it in advance? What if you requested the details to work out the way they did, and they happen, precisely as you had hoped for, and not just once but many times? Is that just all coincidence?

What if you received a warning in advance of something about to go wrong, without asking for it, and because you listened and took action, you avoided what could have been a disaster? Is that just a gut feeling?

What if in the heat of the moment with only a few seconds to spare, a specific memory comes to mind that saves you from having a tragedy that could have been fatal? Is that just instinct, even though you've never performed that act before?

Are all these occurrences just fate or the luck of the draw? Is your gut able to see the future, even when there is no evidence in the present? What if a person experiences *divine intervention* many times, over decades, in a multitude of ways? Would you then begin to think that there is more to this than just random luck?

If you accept that *divine intervention* is real, but you can't recall some or any specific accounts in your life that you are sure of, perhaps all you need to do is ask, and they will be brought to your remembrance. When we open our minds to that possibility, it can open our eyes to see that it has been happening all along, but we've passed it off as luck or ignored it altogether. My challenge to you would be; to ask the source of *divine intervention* in your life, to reveal it to you, and remind you of how active it has been throughout your life and then be patient and see what comes to mind.

## But Why Do Skeptics Claim It Isn't Real?

Throughout history, many recorded events allude to the presence of some entity that is all-knowing and all-loving, which has provided help for humanity. There are also accounts of beings described as angels, who provided guidance in a crisis and then vanished. Are those many millions of accounts just fantasizing or misinterpretation, as in the opinion of a skeptic?

It's easy for skeptics to write off historical accounts because there are no eyewitnesses around to verify what they saw. But that doesn't mean that it didn't happen. A skeptic is forming an opinion based on doubt and not having enough evidence to declare something as true or false. It just means that the skeptic has no personal experience with it.

They have formed an opinion based on a lack of personal knowledge, which they feel should apply to everyone else, despite the firsthand accounts of others to the contrary. They choose to disregard the experiences of others, in order to support their disbelief, as that's a more comfortable path for them to take than to try and understand why they haven't seen it in their own lives.

They base their conclusion on not experiencing any facts for themselves, and then declare that it could not and has not existed for anyone else throughout history. That is the height of arrogance, as the life experience of a skeptic who has never recognized *divine intervention* for themselves, cannot make a credible judgement for the millions of people who genuinely have experienced it, and recognized it for what it was.

Would you accept the opinion of a plumber, shoe salesman, factory worker, or lawyer as credible, if each is declaring to you what it is like to travel in outer space? Would you accept their opinion over that of an astronaut who has experienced it? Any logical person would say "no," as personal experience holds far more credibility than speculation, and the theories of anyone who has never experienced it.

Why then does anyone listen to the opinion of a skeptic who has never experienced *divine intervention*, who then declares that it is just in your imagination? Especially when they have not walked in your shoes, and witnessed what you have?

In reality the opinion of a skeptic, without personal evidence, has very little value if any. Just declaring one's self a skeptic, seems to be their badge of honour. But in reality, it exposes the fact that they not only have no evidence, but that they are unwilling to accept any evidence presented to them—in essence claiming to be a skeptic, is saying one is willfully blind.

## How Do You Access 'Divine Intervention' In Your Life?

This is really a *two-part* question, based on what you believe the character of God is, and how you communicate! Also bear in mind that my opinions are based on my understanding of having a Christian's relationship with God, as I do not have the background in other religions to judge them or offer an opinion.

The answer to the *first part* of the question is to develop a correct understanding of how, when, and why a Divine Entity would choose to interact in your life. And that requires a clearer understanding of the nature of God.

If you asked 100 random believers what or who God is, you would probably get close to 100 slightly different answers, as it's based primarily on their upbringing and what others have taught them. It can often not be the result of personal experience for many of them.

Let me give you an example. Some might confuse the image of a beneficial Creator helping humanity, with those who believe that God is impatient and easily angered. Throughout history, many have alleged that God is jealous and spiteful, and requires a considerable sacrifice to win his favour, or even a human sacrifice to be appeased. Also, that God will easily decide to destroy you or cast you aside, forever, when witnessing your slightest transgression. This action, of course maintains a relationship of abject fear, guilt, and slavery, and not a relationship built upon love, gratitude, and acceptance.

Those negative characteristics attributed to God are also the worst characteristics of humanity, as described in most sacred writings. Why then, would a God who says that we must rid ourselves of those negative characteristics, actually behave like that, as an example to us? That would make God out to be an incredible hypocrite—and nothing could justify that kind of behaviour from an entity that is supposed to exemplify the greatest of compassion, patience, love, and forgiveness.

So, a problem exists in the different images that can be settled only through a greater understanding. People have, in many cases, created an image of God that suits a particular human mindset for their own purposes. You must decide for yourself how you will view a Divine Entity interacting in your life, and the best way to come to a full understanding is through personal experience.

Throughout my life, I've had many encounters with *divine intervention*. The most significant ones in the early years occurred after I became a Christian, in the last couple of months of high school, in 1975. Those initial experiences mostly took place in Edmonton and Hinton, Alberta, while going to Forestry School. In all of those events, I was guided by an unseen force, which I referred to as God, providing *divine intervention* precisely when I needed it.

I also need to point out that when looking back, I had many encounters with *divine intervention* before 1975. But I never recognized the source at the time. So, becoming a Christian did not determine God's care and compassion for me; it merely allowed me to see it more clearly. In short, becoming a Christian is not a prerequisite for receiving God's love or attention to the circumstances in our lives where we need help. It just helped me recognize it when it occurred, and that was my journey to take.

In my opinion, and of course, my opinion only affects me; the Spirit of God isn't as concerned with the correct terminology you may or may not use as much as God is concerned with your attitude and honesty.

Some church denominations may *claim* that you must present yourself in a posture of humility and should be kneeling to pray or to talk to God. Others may say that you must pray with your eyes closed, or even with your eyes open, or you need to wave your hands in the air and sing praises to get God's attention before you can make your petition.

Some may say you need to light a candle, or repeat a sequence of memorized prayers, or recite passages of sacred texts while handling prayer beads. Others will spin a prayer wheel to earn merit and help them focus on specific prayers. Some will carry a small cross, or a tiny figurine, or kiss the feet of a large statue in the image of a deity or saint. Some will tell you that you must give money to the church to receive God's blessing. Then, of course, some will *claim* that another person, who is placed in authority by the church, must be the one to pray for you, as God will listen to them, much more willingly than he will listen to you.

Another practice is to sit in meditation for hours and focus on God and listen to your breathing, while you burn incense, to reach a higher state of consciousness. Some choose to chant a mantra, that they believe will bring them closer to God and make a connection with the Universe.

Are any of these acts wrong? I would suggest it depends on your thinking process and why you are engaging in them and what is the focus of your devotion.

Are you imagining that God is actually embodied in the artifacts you focus on for worship? Then I would question what or who you think

God really is, as you may be assuming you can merit God's *grace* by your actions.

Then, of course, there's the other side to a relationship with what or who people view is God, that being the concept of penance—where individuals attempt to impress God with their sacrifice. Some will travel miles on their knees or prostrate on their bellies, or even whip themselves with a lash till they bleed. Some will deny relationships and abandon their wives and children or take a vow of silence to show how devoted they are to God. In the most extreme cases, they will undergo painful body mutilations and piercings or even get nailed to a cross in an attempt to prove their loyalty to God. They seem to believe that they need to punish themselves, to try and earn God's favour or find forgiveness. But is that what a loving and forgiving God is all about?

Does God revel in the satisfaction of seeing humanity suffer? What kind of a God would enjoy watching that? To me, these punitive actions reduce the image and the Spirit of a loving God to the cruelest and most debased works of humanity.

And we are back again to the question of, "Does God think and act like a man does, and is God susceptible to all the negative characteristics we are supposed to rid ourselves from?" If the answer is "no," then we must question the effectiveness of these acts at trying to earn God's favour.

It's just my opinion, but I believe that many of those protocols are created by humans, whether by prophets, priests, popes, pastors, or any number of authoritarian figures. And not necessarily are they dictated by God, especially those where punishment is the path to a spiritual relationship. These precepts exist to make the person feel they have paid a debt or took part in the act of reverence, and are now justified to feel more worthy and will be successful in their efforts to interact with God. I believe many of these methods exist only to exact control over the hopeful, who look to those in authority for guidance and approval. I don't think that any of those methods or actions are an absolute requirement in a relationship with God!

Continued repetition of prayers or sacred texts, may strengthen the resolve of believers and make you feel better about your relationship with God, building your sense of devotion in communicating with God. But I can also tell you that a person cannot wear down God's reluctance to grant your petition, simply by continually repeating specific phrases or engaging in certain acts.

If one thinks that repetition is an effective way to coerce God to act on your behalf, they are mistaken. That is having the belief that, if you say it enough times or repeat the act enough times, then God must act in your favour, whether it is to grant you something material, or even if it is to have God forgive you.

People may not realize it, but that kind of thinking reduces the personality of God, to be subservient to your actions. It's the belief that God is actually under your authority and that you can control the Spirit of God, forcing it to do your bidding. In essence, you think God now owes you, because of your sacrifice or devotion!

That kind of thinking never forces God to do anything. Yes, those methods are staunchly defended by some religious leaders who promote them. But keep in mind that they are telling you those things for a reason, and it is not to control God's actions to work on your behalf; because you cannot control God, it is to control you!

I can tell you from personal experience that God listens to the smallest voice or merely the thoughts and feelings you express. There is no physical demonstration required to get God's attention or to earn the right to communicate with God. That is because God's love is never based on your actions, although that is the teaching of many.

Sometimes we are taught that the more you give to God, the more God has to give to you.

However, God's blessings aren't as a result of what you can do for God, as that would suggest we could buy God's goodwill if we just find the right price, and that simply isn't the case. God's love is unconditional and is always there, but we separate ourselves from it by our own choices in life. In essence, we walk away from God; God never walks away from us.

God's care for you and acts of *divine intervention* are based on God's *grace,* not on your merit, through earning it with your actions, whatever form they may take. That said, when we are more attuned to the Spirit of God in our lives, we are more willing to listen to God's direction and guidance, and be generous with our resources to help others. And by listening to the spirit, we do not put ourselves in a compromising situation that we will regret later.

The physical action you might engage in, or the position of the body, does not impress God enough to warrant attention. This is because there is only one perfect way to attract God's attention.

God listens to and never rejects an honest and unselfish heart!

I'm referring to the truth of your innermost thoughts! You don't even have to speak the words out loud, or even say them more than once for God to hear you. Which has been proven to me many times over, and you will read about those circumstances in my stories.

If anyone is telling you that you have to say certain words in proper order or do specific actions or give a certain amount for God to notice you, that's a result of their view of the character of God. A person can be kneeling at the altar or even lying flat on the floor in front of a church full of people or jumping up and down in worship waving their arms in the air. Or they can have the evangelist, priest, pastor or deacons and elders of the church laying hands on them in prayer.

All of those things are fine and acceptable to God. But I can tell you that God will not pay any more attention to them than the person sitting in the back, which has a humble heart and honestly asks God for help, or to intervene in someone else's life. Or the penniless and homeless person sitting on the curb, feeling lost and unloved, and reaches out to God, to send someone along who cares enough to help.

I'm not saying that those acts are wrong when communicating with God if that is your choice. If you feel comfortable addressing God in that fashion, then that's the way it works for you, providing it works, of course, and your thinking is in the right place. But if you don't feel comfortable with a particular type of behaviour, then don't do it, just because someone else is. Or because you might feel out of place or ostracized if you don't conform to what everyone else is doing. You need to understand the heart of God if you want a personal relationship.

If you're trying to prove to people that you fit in, by bowing to pressure from others who have a different view of the character of God, it may make you feel uncomfortable. If you are being judged by others for the way you relate to God, then find a place where you do feel comfortable. Communication with God is not about pleasing other people, who don't accept you unconditionally. Or trying to impress God with how righteous you are, since in the Christian faith, no one has superseded the example that Jesus set, to impress God. Have your actions topped that?

God always accepts you unconditionally and wants you to come as you are. No pretense, no false humility, and no demonstrations are required in an attempt to impress. God only wants to help you feel better about yourself and will try and guide you into a closer relationship to accomplish that. In that process, you will have choices to make as you begin to treat yourself better, in ways that will uplift you. And not treating yourself in ways that make you feel like you aren't a good person to yourself or others, or make you feel unworthy of God's love and care.

With that said, of course, we still need to be respectful of those around us. We should not intentionally disregard their sensitivities, making them feel uncomfortable by the way we act or dress, as that reflects on our pride and ego. That should not be what you are there for if you genuinely want to communicate with God, and fellowship with others in a similar setting. Each of us is here to travel this earthly journey and fulfill a divine purpose, in fellowship with others, and that requires respect for them and their beliefs, even if you disagree with them.

The *second part* of the question depends on whether you believe in God, or even accept that *divine intervention* exists or you reject both. Your belief or rejection should not rely on the unrealistic image or expectations you may have of people who say that they do follow scripture and believe in God. Because when you see that they do not live perfect lives, you may reject it all as being false.

However, declaring something to be false, simply because of the bad behaviour of some, who claim to practice that faith, and follow those scriptures, is quite illogical. That's like saying that all doctors are quacks, and all medical science is fake, because of the fatal errors of some bad practitioners, and you will never go to any doctor again. A recent Johns Hopkins study found that more than 250,000 people in the USA die every year from medical malpractice. Other reports *claim* the numbers to be as high as 440,000.

Yet, who do you go and see when you or your loved ones are sick or injured? You call on members of that same fraternity that was responsible for all those unnecessary deaths. That's because you realize that those fatal mistakes do not represent all doctors, hospitals, or medical schools, or that it renders their literature invalid.

You just have to find someone that you can trust, to feel confident that you are receiving sound advice. And what is the best way to determine the ones you can trust, for sound advice about God, or to discover if *divine intervention* is real? If someone has directed you to or given you this book to read, that person would be an excellent place to start. They may also direct you to someone with more knowledge and personal experience with God. A person you can meet with, who can guide you closer to the truth, and help you along in your journey of discovery.

## Already A Believer but Would Like More Evidence?

For people who claim they already are believers in a loving God, they need to ask themselves if they believe in a personal God. Or, do they have faith in what someone else had told them to think about God? Of course, in the beginning, that's what our experience is, right? When someone has shared their faith with us, we have accepted that as truth, have embraced it, and started our journey of personal discovery. The final goal of any trip is the destination. For the lives of believers, that's when we leave this world.

But any journey will have way-points along the route that bring us closer to our destination. They keep us on track and build our faith and confidence that we are on the right path. That's what acts of *divine intervention* create for us.

If your belief or faith is based only upon the opinions of others, how do you know that their advice comes from personal experience and fact? Are they just repeating what they've heard as well, and have never personally experienced God? What I am getting at is this; each person needs to experience God for themselves. You should not go through life merely believing the opinions of others, because those people may let you down. If your faith in God is based solely on your image of another person, who you look up to, then it is not based on your personal experience.

Many, if not most atheists, *claim* that they have embraced their belief because they do not see any evidence of there being a God. Later in this book, I talk about why one does not understand what they are looking for and why they are not able to see the obvious. Briefly, though; if you don't know what to look for, or refuse to accept valid evidence when it's presented, then it's quite apparent that in your opinion, no evidence exists. But remember, it is just your opinion, and it doesn't change reality as you are basing your opinion on a lack of evidence, not on an abundance of evidence.

That's like saying that you don't believe any life exists below 1,800 metres (5,900 feet) in the ocean since no light penetrates below that depth. That was the scientifically accepted position of biologists for many decades because they believed that all life required sunlight. They didn't have the evidence they sought and so believed they were 100 percent correct! Did their opinion change reality? No, it didn't!

Life existed in abundance deep in the ocean, they just couldn't see it, and the opinion they formed beforehand, precluded them from even looking for it. Today, we believe it exists because someone else has seen the evidence of it in videos captured by cameras on deep-diving submersibles. Yet, although 99.99 percent of the population has never witnessed deep ocean life, for themselves, from within these submersibles, we still accept the fact that it is real because someone else says it is, and they witnessed it.

And so, it is, with recognizing an act of *divine intervention*. Some people, if not most, will need to experience it in their own lives, to believe it exists. Or, at the very least, read about the events in the lives of others, whom they trust to be truthful, and then choose to open their minds to the possibilities and experiences.

If they choose not to even look for it because they have already arrived at an opinion that it doesn't exist, does that mean it doesn't exist? Absolutely NOT! It just means it will not exist for that person, even if it is evident to everyone else. There is nothing more restricting in life for a person than to have a skeptical mind that is closed to experiencing reality for themself and not allowing their minds to be opened!

# Recognizing 'Divine Intervention' In Your Life

Once you do consider the possibility, you may be reminded of a circumstance that you have already experienced, which was indeed *divine intervention*. You had simply passed it off as just good luck. Becoming aware of it is an act of sensitizing your mind to the moment of *divine intervention,* allowing you to recognize it when it happens again? Being able to identify it would then allow you to write those encounters down as a reminder.

It's good to be reminded of past events, that you now recognize as *divine intervention*, because it is essential to your wellbeing and your relationships as you go through life, facing the daily trials of living.

When a person has various difficulties coping with daily struggle and heartbreak, everything seems dark around them, and the future can look bleak. That person needs hope to carry on. When feeling broken and heavy-burdened, there often appears to be no way to overcome the troubles, and hope is lost. But, if you can recall how God has provided for you in the past, it will remind you that you are never going through life's struggles alone, and help from God is just a thought away. Keeping a journal will help bring these events to your mind when times are tough, and you feel that stress and anxiety are crushing you.

If God had intervened in the past when you needed help, why not now? Having a written record also makes it easier to share with someone else who is going through similar struggles, too. And you can provide hope for them to be patient and ask for help when they needed it.


## A Final Note of Encouragement

I hope that through describing these experiences in my life, it will provide you with some insight into how, when, where, and why *divine intervention* takes place. Also, that it doesn't have to be a miraculous earth-shattering event. It can be a gentle act or a seemingly small circumstance, but knowing that it still matters enough for *divine intervention* to act on your behalf; will give you confidence that you matter to God.

After you read this book, I hope you feel some comfort and assurance that you are not going through this life alone, or that you think you have to face all of its struggles by yourself. Be assured that there is always someone watching over you, willing to help if you let them! And if you know of someone else who is searching for God or seeking the truth about the possibilities that *divine intervention* is real, I hope you will share this book with them.

In these real-life stories I share, I have taken the time to set the stage for you and describe a little background. This extra detail is so that you may understand my mindset and the circumstances I was going through at the time, rather than me just saying I prayed for this or that, and the answer came. I have done it this way so that people might be able to identify with something in their own lives that they might be going through. Also, for you to then realize that if God worked it out for someone else, it could work out for you as well.

May you find a blessing and some encouragement in the stories that follow!

# CHAPTER TWO

# I'll Be Content

In the fall of 1977, after I had gotten married in July and finished my summer job at the Swan River Conservation office in Manitoba, my wife and I moved out of that flee and cockroach-infested apartment above a grocery store, and returned to Alberta. A good friend of mine, Verne S., who had also been the best man at our wedding, knew we were coming back to Alberta. By chance or providence (I think it was *divine intervention*), he had met Carl O'Leary. He had been the photogrammetry instructor at the Forestry School in Hinton, Alberta, which I had attended with Verne. Carl was involved in setting up the Alberta Government's Phase III mapping program for the province, to remap its forest cover.

Verne mentioned that I was looking for a job, and Carl said I could come in for an interview, so I did. I got the position with Resource Evaluation and Planning as they had only started up and needed people with photogrammetry training and forestry experience. I was never very good at using a stereoscope in school, I thought, but it turned out that I had a natural gift for it. In fact, within three months, I was interpreting, on average, 130 square miles of forest cover every month, which would be about 337 square kilometres. The standard they expected for each person to work up to in six months was 60 square miles per month (155 sq. km), and many in the group were struggling to reach that level.

At about the time I was hired, there was a glitch and a change of departments that made me the lowest-paid forest technician in the office. Those employed before and after me were making ten percent more than I was. I also was doing twice the work. Because I was so fast at my job, my work became highly scrutinized in the field. From actual field audits, they discovered that I had over 85 percent accuracy in determining heights, ages, species composition, densities, and understories down to 2 hectares (5 acres) in size, from looking at the forest cover on aerial photographs at a scale of four inches to one mile. There was no one else in the group that attained more than 60 percent accuracy from the ground analysis conducted in the field by forestry staff.

Eventually, the quota for the rest of the group had been increased to 80 square miles (207 sq. km) per month, as they noticed that people always stayed slightly below their requirements. When a group of Russian forestry officials toured our offices, our manager standing near my desk, bragged to them that our accuracy rate was above 85 percent with a production capacity of 130 square miles per person per month. Yeah, sure I thought, I was producing that per month, but no one else came close, and I was the lowest paid.

I kept up this pace for two years, never getting wage parity with staff that I was now training and evaluating their work. I had so much surplus area banked that I could have stopped working for months and still hand in my 337 square kilometres (130 sq. miles) every month. So, they farmed me out to other departments to do field studies, while I continued to hand in my double production every month. Have you ever felt underappreciated—I have! My ego was also hurting because I knew how much more effort, I was putting in than the rest and not receiving compensation for it.

I finally had enough after my fourth work evaluation with another promise that if I just kept it up for another six months, I'd get parity—I'd heard that before. You can only feel used and taken advantage of for so long before you realize it's time to leave.

Then, it came—that proverbial straw that broke the camel's back. My supervisor, Richard, said he was not going to approve my expense account. It was only around $210 and covered three nights in the hotel and meals, which I had paid for during a fieldwork trip in Northern Alberta. He said he would approve it if I increased my 130 square miles per month. No other employees were forced even to come up to my level of production. I decided that blackmail was the last straw, and I left that job.

They were rather angry that their top producer had walked away. Especially since they were well behind their mandated production levels for the project, but it was no longer my problem. You never know what you missed until it's gone, I thought, but I didn't see how this would turn out, or apply to me.

I took a job with a friend framing houses. And after three months, I discovered that the contractor was a crook and was going to get sued for his illegal actions. He told both of us that we wouldn't get paid. That meant a lot less income than missing the ten percent parity from my previous job, and one's ego takes a beating. We were expecting our first child, and I was desperate for a job. So late one night, I was walking around the soccer field across from our apartment and talking to God. I demanded he give me employment the next day, and I didn't want to wait any longer.

The next morning, while looking through the job ads section in the newspaper, I found one for a structural steel draftsman at Rhodes Vaughn. This company supplied shaped rebar to all construction sites in the province. I went there and applied and got the job. They hired me simply because I knew how to use a drafting table, not because I knew anything about rebar or structural drafting. It turns out their last recruit had just quit, and that should have been a *warning* sign to me. The guy that was going to train me was only there for another few days, and then he quit, too, leaving me to deal with the management.

How does the saying go? "They were as crooked as a barrel of fishhooks and lower than a snake's belly in a wagon rut!"

*First* off, they offered me a monthly salary of 25 percent less than I had been getting at the government as a photo interpreter and resource technician, and indeed it was minimum wage. That hurt, and it tended to make a person feel a little humble about their abilities.

*Secondly*, they continually talked about how they could rip off the place and clean it out in one day, then be gone before anyone found out. So, I was concerned about getting caught up in a police investigation as well.

The *third* reason I had my doubts about working for them was after they had a little too much to drink at the Christmas party, which consisted of a few bottles of booze and doughnuts in the 10x40 foot work-trailer that was their entire office. They confided that they had changed their names when they fled Nova Scotia.

And the *fourth* reason, as if I needed another, was that they were also planning on concocting a story to fire the yard foreman on their site, who was the younger brother of the manager of the Calgary Rhodes Vaughn office so that he couldn't spy on them.

To say, I was *miserable* working there— would be an understatement, but I had put myself into this mess, and I had no one else to blame. I realized one day that it was my pride and discontent that had put me here, and unless that changed, I wouldn't get out of this mess. My drafting table was separated from the front desk by one of those rectangle movable partitions, with a cloth facing on it. So, without anyone seeing me one afternoon, I knelt behind my desk and accepted responsibility for my situation. I recognized I had put myself here because of my attitude and pride and unwillingness to stand up for myself in my government job and demand parity. Then my impatience to wait for God to bring me a job I wanted. I had to surrender my will, and I said that I would be happy here until something better comes along, and I meant it!

After that revelation, confession, and commitment, I felt a bit of the anxiety had left me, and I went back to work. Within about half an hour, I was trying to think of the forest companies we had heard about in school, and I was wondering if they had any forest technician jobs coming up. The only name that came to mind was Swanson Lumber, out of the dozens we had visited or learned about, and I don't know why I couldn't remember any of the rest. So, I got the phone book out and looked them up, thinking they had an office in Swan Hills, Alberta. After calling there, I found out their corporate office was in Edmonton. So, I gave them a phone call and asked if they had any summer jobs in forestry coming available for forest technicians.

They asked me what I was currently doing, and I told them. I also added that I had two years as a photo interpreter with the Resource Evaluation and Planning Department of the Government. I was their highest producing photo interpreter for all that time. The receptionist told me to hang on for a minute, and then a gentleman came on the phone and asked me to repeat my credentials, which I did.

He then said that they were planning to do a forest assessment on aerial photography of an area they were thinking of applying for an FMA (Forest Management Agreement). He then stated that they needed an aerial photo interpreter to assess it, and could I come in tomorrow, Thursday, for an interview at 4 p.m. What do you think I said?

I was ecstatic, but I wasn't sure how I would get the time off to make it there. It was a 45-minute drive to the south side of the city from the very north side where I worked, it would be rush hour, and I usually didn't get off until 5 p.m. So, I asked for help to work it out somehow, and left it to God that day.

The next morning, I still had no clue how I would get to the interview, and then just before noon, the office manager, (the wife of the manager, a corrupt pair if there ever were) wanted to leave early that day, so we closed up at 3 p.m. And I was off to Swanson Lumber.

Arriving at their office on time, I met the people in charge, and they gave me some aerial photography to study. I didn't even need a stereoscope as I could see in stereo without using one, and quickly delineated the forest stands for them in just a few minutes. After their Forester had a look at them and gave his approval, the manager then said that they had hired someone from the

Resource Evaluation Branch for this job, but that person, John B., had decided to take a month off and go to the Caribbean before starting.

Swanson Lumber wanted to start right now as millions of dollars were at stake. He asked if I could start on Monday, and of course, I said, "yes." He then asked what I was making for salary—I hesitated to say I was only making $775 a month.

So, he said, "Probably around $1,200, which is roughly what Resource Evaluation staff made."—I nodded in agreement that "yes," that's what they made at the time. He then said, "I think we can do better; how about $1,550 a month?"

I kept a straight face and said, "That sounds okay," but I was doing summersaults inside.

How do you think that made me feel? And it only happened after I said I would be content with where I was until God brought along something better. My life changed in half an hour after that point of accepting responsibility for my situation, without excuses. How can that be a coincidence?

I had no idea Swanson Lumber was even doing an inventory, let alone that they had hired someone who took a month to go on vacation. By the way, I knew John B., and I used to evaluate his work before I had caught him fudging it all, so Swanson Lumber definitely wouldn't have gotten their monies worth from him.

I now had another problem though, how do I ensure I get paid by my current manager as I knew he had held back pay from other people. They had even cancelled payment at the bank for cheques on people who had quit on them. Then they would tell upper management that they had caught them stealing or some other made-up excuse and had to fire them so they wouldn't get paid. We couldn't make rent if I didn't get my last two weeks of pay.

I went to work the next day, Friday, with a resignation letter written up, but knowing that as soon as I gave it to them, the last two weeks of work would have been for free. So, I asked God for help, and since everything else was working out, maybe this would too. At noon, the office manager asked me to run to the bank in St. Albert for her and make deposits. Okay, no problem, I thought, and as I was about to leave, she said, "Oh, and here's your paycheque, too," and I was out the door.

When I got to their bank to make the Rhodes Vaughn deposits, I asked the teller if I could cash a company paycheque here as well. No problem, she said and counted out the cash for my earnings. I returned to the office. Then went to the steelyard first and talked to the foreman, who was the brother of the manager in the Calgary office. I told him that they planned on firing him so that he couldn't spy on them; he said he would call his brother. I went to the office trailer with a smile. I handed her the deposit books and my letter of resignation. Then I was out the door and off the lot in a couple of minutes.

The manager had already been calling my wife at home and threatening her, saying that I'd better get back there right now or there'd be hell to pay. When he called again, I waited while he unleashed a barrage of insults and threats, and then I told him what I had said to the guy they were planning to fire. I also told him that I was waiting for a call from Calgary as they wanted details, which was true. With this, he hung up, and I found out, they both resigned that next Monday!

I hadn't planned to affect their lives, but I wasn't going to be threatened and especially would not allow my wife to be harassed by corrupt managers either. I was very thankful for *divine intervention*, and that it worked everything out for me in a total of three days from when I surrendered my will, my pride, and ego to God. So, did I learn from this—well, yes, for a while, but I'll tell you what happened a decade later, further along in this book.

# CHAPTER THREE

# Didn't Want High Level

During the six months I worked on the contract for Swanson Lumber, we had bought a new condominium in the northeast end of Edmonton and also had our first child, a little blue-eyed boy. As the project for Swanson Lumber was drawing to a close, the management came to me and asked if I would move up to High Level, Alberta, and work as a forest technician for their lumber mill. There is nothing wrong with High Level, Alberta, of course, except that it is 740 kilometres (460 miles) north of Edmonton and only 177 kilometres (110 miles) from the Northwest Territories border. It would put my wife many hours away from her family, and it was quite a small town back in 1980. We'd have to drive a long way for any decent shopping as there was no such thing as Amazon Prime delivery back then.

My wife didn't want to go, so I declined their offer and wasn't sure what else I could get for a job. After praying about it, a gentleman came to mind who worked for the Federal Ministry of Forests at an office in Edmonton. I made a phone call, and he told me that there was a guy in the city this week that was conducting a Forest Inventory and Habitat Assessment in the Liard River Basin in the lower portion of the Yukon, for the Federal Government, and was interviewing companies.

Do you believe that it was just luck that after I prayed for guidance, I happened to think of the name of the only guy who would know about this project? And that the Yukon Forest Service representative (which was federal jurisdiction) was in Edmonton that week to interview companies; then you have far more faith in pure luck than I do, and you are missing the point. But as you read more encounters I had with *divine intervention*; you will understand the significance.

I got his telephone number, made contact, and met him in a hotel room where he showed me a sample of the aerial photography and the extent of the project area. I then had to come up with a bid for the project and get back to him in two days. He said they had already more or less settled on another contractor, and didn't say who it was, but would wait for my input. I went home and worked on costs for helicopter charter, hotel rooms, and travel expenses, and then for the delineation of the aerial photography and classification of the vegetation, and gave him a price I thought would work out for me.

It turned out to be about 50 percent less than the next bid, which I found out was also from two guys at Resource Evaluation and Planning who had been chastised and penalized for fraudulent work on the Alberta Inventory, while I was still there. I had caught what they were doing while being asked by the manager to audit their work, but the government couldn't afford to fire any photo interpreters since they were so far behind their deadlines.

I wasn't intending to steal any work from them as I didn't even know they were bidding on it, and just like Swanson Lumber, it comes down to both price and availability, and my rate was much better, and they couldn't start for another couple of months. Besides that, I was a husband and new father, and both of those guys were single without the responsibilities I had, and I couldn't feel bad about it.

So, after one prayer for help and one name provided, I bid on another contract and won it, all within less than a week. That act of *divine intervention* carried us through for another eight- or nine-months' time. I completed the project and got to fly a large section of the southern Yukon in the process and conduct fieldwork, and it went well.

Then I was faced with the same situation of needing another job and not knowing where to look, so I prayed about it.

# CHAPTER FOUR

# The Condominium

After the project for the Yukon ended, there were a couple of months of no income, so it was getting tight financially, and I was worrying. I then wondered if I could get a job with the Alberta Government as a Forest Officer and contacted the only person I knew in the Ministry of Forests and asked to meet. We had a short interview in his office, and he said I'd have no problem getting a position, but it would mean moving out of the city.

He contacted me a day later and said that I could accept a forest officer's position in Whitecourt, Alberta, but had to be there by the end of the month. That was, of course, exciting, as I had a permanent job offer. Then a couple of days later, I heard from the Whitecourt Forest, and they were only going to offer me a summer job as a forest technician, so it would only be temporary employment.

This job-offer presented a real problem for us as we had a mortgage on our condo and certainly couldn't pay rent in Whitecourt as well as payments in Edmonton until it sold. What if I am unemployed after the summer in a small town where work was hard to get? I was also concerned about moving out of the city and not sure if this was the right thing to do or not. I doubted my judgement on the issue; I needed more guidance and confirmation, so I put up a *fleece*. For those who aren't familiar, the term "relates to a story in the Bible in which a man needed direction, so he asked God to do a specific task."

Here's the story in Judges 6:36-40:

> Then Gideon said to God, "If You will deliver Israel [a]through me, as You have spoken, 37 behold, I will put a fleece of wool on the threshing floor. If there is dew on the fleece only, and it is dry on all the ground, then I will know that You will deliver Israel [b]through me, as You have spoken." When he arose early the next morning and squeezed the fleece, he drained a bowl full of water from the fleece. 39 Then Gideon said to God, please let me make a test once more with the fleece, let it now be dry only on the fleece, and let there

be dew on all the ground." 40 God did so that night; for it was dry only on the fleece, and dew was on all the ground.

So, the principle being—if you need further confirmation about the direction before you, and if it is the one God intended, then you can put up a *fleece* to make sure. But, here's the caveat; you must commit in your heart that you will trust the answer; however, it turns out, and that's the direction you will take. It does you no good to ignore the results of the *fleece* and continue in your own judgement. Or to have pre-determined in your mind what direction you will take despite what the *fleece* tells you. Believe me, because I have done it both ways and saw the results of having my mind already established in a particular direction, ignoring the warnings and then watching it turn out badly in the long run.

Since I didn't know for sure about taking the job and having to move, I decided to put up a *fleece*, that being the sale of our condominium. I said to God, "If you want me to take the job in Whitecourt, then you have to sell our home before the end of the month."

The Edmonton Journal newspaper had hundreds of ads for condominiums for sale, so what are the chances that ours would sell within three weeks? Very slim, I thought. Our advertisement came out in the Journal that Saturday and that evening we received a telephone call from someone interested. A couple came over on Sunday and looked at it and offered us our asking price. On Monday, they closed the deal and brought over a cheque, so there was no backing out now.

How's that for answering my request for heavenly guidance, by asking God to show his will and answering my *fleece*? Out of literally well over a hundred condominium ads for sale, ours sold on the first business day after the advertisement came out. Just a coincidence, you might say, well for me, I don't believe so?

In the last week of the month, we drove to Whitecourt and found a one-bedroom apartment to rent on the third floor, and then rented a U-Haul to move our possessions. I loaded and unloaded it all by myself and carried everything up the three flights of stairs, including the bed, couch, and deep freeze. We were finally starting a new chapter.

# CHAPTER FIVE

# Let the Air Out

Some time had passed, and I'm now living in Whitecourt, Alberta, with my wife and my little boy. I was working as a Forest Officer for the Alberta Forest Service since they gave me a forest officer's position just two months after starting there with a summer job as a forest technician. Many things had transpired that had proven to me over and over that *divine intervention* is undeniably real.

A lot of those events centered on the sport of hunting. However, I have separated those stories for another book that may have more appeal to folks that enjoy providing meat for their family and have kept this one for evidence of *divine intervention* in other aspects of life. Feel free to have a look at the other book and share it with men and women who enjoy the outdoors and hunting and either already know God, or you'd like to share an aspect of God with them, that involves their sport. (For availability on this and other books, please visit phaelonpublishing.ca).

I am not sure of the year, maybe 1982; we had lovely friends in Whitecourt. And the Ryks' family, who had three daughters, and loved our little boy; offered to babysit him whenever we asked, so on one occasion in early November, we left him at their place. My wife and I took our hunting vehicle—our only vehicle, a two-door Toyota Tercel car, to a rugged area about one-hour northwest of Whitecourt and at the dead-end of an abandoned road. We had to descend a very long steep hill, being around 300 metres (330 yards) in length and at about a 20 percent grade to get into the area. Once down there, we walked further into the bush, and I tried calling for elk from there.

We didn't have any success hunting, and as it was getting late, we decided to leave, especially since it had started to drizzle a bit. The temperature had dropped considerably, and we also had quite a long drive to get back. So, we walked back to the car to head for home. The steep grade of the hill in question started only about 137 metres (150 yards) from the end of the road where we parked, and I could only build up so much speed to try and make it up but was confident I could. Unfortunately, confidence isn't worth squat when nature is against you.

I could only make it about 45 metres (50 yards) up the hill and then began to slide back down. We tried it three times with the same result. What had happened was that the drizzle had frozen on the road surface as the temperature dropped and produced a very greasy surface. No problem I thought, Darlee can drive, and I'll push the car up the hill. Well, as you can imagine, that didn't work. It was so slick that my boots couldn't get any traction on the hard clay of the road. With the slippery ice sheen on the surface and the tires spinning, I was holding most of the weight of the car as the incline got steeper, and that wasn't going to work.

We tried it several times with no success, and I was exhausted and out of options—or so I thought. I started to worry since absolutely no one knew where we were. The only thing they knew was that we were a long way to the northwest on one of the dozens of old abandoned logging roads, and we didn't have a cell phone in the 80s to call anyone. Not that they would work even today, as we were in a bowl near a river, and no cell signal would reach into that area.

So, what do you do in an instance like this? When you cannot make it on your strength, and you're out of ideas? If you had gone through prior situations in life where you asked for help from God and had experienced *divine intervention* many times, you ask for help, of course! But still not anticipating where that help would come from, as no one is going to be driving down this road tonight.

As I stood outside the car, and it again started to drizzle, now mixed with sleet, I considered my options, which ranged between zero and none. Then—I suddenly had such a definite feeling that I should remember something, and the story started to play out in my mind.

In about 1978, when visiting my wife's parents one winter when the roads were icy, her father, Erhard, shared a short story with me that I found fascinating, but then quickly forgot. He had said that in the early 60s, it had rained in December, creating a black ice situation on the highway. The RCMP was stopping vehicles from travelling on Highway 2 between Westlock and Edmonton since the road was impassible.

If you have ever experienced a black ice situation, you will know what I mean. If not, then envision yourself standing on a sheet of ice tilted at an angle with water running over it. That's how slippery black ice is! You literally can't stand upright on it if there is any slope to it at all, let alone a vehicle with spinning tires gaining traction, or staying on the road as no steering was possible.

But Erhard had survived WWII as a young Polish boy of 16. He had been conscripted by the Germans and forced to fight in Italy and France. Finally, he had a chance to break free and surrendered to the allies in France. He then got a job with the British army in England driving truck. He was only 5'4" and had learned many tricks on how to survive under challenging situations and was undoubtedly unwilling to not make it home to his family, just because the RCMP had said it was too dangerous.

What he did was something he had learned a long time ago, and I would bet that most people aren't aware of it today. He got out of his vehicle and let half the air out of his tires equally. Then he got back in and drove around the RCMP vehicles and headed for home with their jaws dropping to the black ice of the pavement. No one could follow him to stop him, because the RCMP couldn't drive on the black ice either, and it hadn't occurred to them that they could increase the tire surface area on the ice, to gain traction by doing this.

Isn't it remarkable how a random story pops into your head from four years previously just when you need it most? And it was initially just something said in a normal conversation that took about three minutes to tell.

I thought what the heck. I have no other choice but to try it, although the flat pavement is not the same as a hill with a 20 percent grade. You have to let the air out evenly. So first, I let out air to a count of ten on each front wheel as it was a front-wheel drive. I had Pirelli radial tires on the car, which are not a very deep tire, to begin with. Darlee drove, and I pushed, and again we slid back down to the starting spot in short order.

Okay, do we declare that story a bust, because it didn't seem to work? That would be the response of most people. But since we didn't have an Option B, what else could we do but let out more air and try again. The second time produced the same results, and I was getting anxious. So, one more time, I let out air to a count of ten. By now, the 35-pound air pressure capacity of the tires was down to about 12 pounds each.

Darlee stepped on the gas, and I was going to push. Well, that didn't work because after about 2 metres (6 feet) of me again pushing, I fell to my knees as she shot up that hill *like a demon was chasing her*. She didn't stop by the way until she was at the top. It was already dark before I made it up that hill, slipping and sliding, but believe me, I didn't mind.

The only problem then was that a big bulldozer had travelled down the main logging road, while we were off on the abandoned side road. It had left large clods of mud on the surface from its tracks, and they had started to freeze. We only had about two inches of rubber below the rims, and it was a very slow and bumpy ride to get back to the pavement.

Ever since then, I've carried a small air compressor to be able to pump up the tires again after I had to use this technique. And I have used it often over the years, even bogged down in a 4x4 in mud but especially on ice and snow. I also now only buy tall tires so that when I let enough air out to have traction, I still have enough air in them to move without damaging the rims.

Those thin profile tires that people buy as a fashion statement on their cars today will never be on any vehicle I own.

So, where was the *divine intervention*? First of all, I had to wonder if the rain and sudden drop in temperature occurred to strand us there for this specific event to unfold. Maybe it was going to happen anyway, and my guardian angel used it as a teaching experience for me to bring things to my remembrance when I needed to get out of a jam. And how about Erhard telling that story to me years before and never mentioning it again? A story implanted in my memory, so it was available to bring forth in this specific emergency. As I would never have thought of doing that on my own, and most people reading this story wouldn't think of it either, have you?

When people drive in the winter, the train of thought is to put some 50-pound sandbags in the trunk for better traction. All it is doing is flattening the drive wheels a tiny bit because 45 kilograms (100 pounds) on a 1,130-kilogram (2,500-pound) vehicle is nothing. Funnier yet, is that people with front-wheel-drive cars still add sandbags to the trunk, providing less traction on their drive wheels. But if you flatten the tires by letting some of the air out, you can climb a hill on ice. Just make sure you can pump them up again, or drive real slow getting to a place where you can pump them up. Too much rapid flexing for too long will overheat them and destroy the sidewalls when they delaminate, so carry that air compressor.

When you are in a jam and need help, ask for it—and be patient. Then clear your mind and see what comes to you, and act upon it. It just might be Divine guidance, trying to help you out.

So, would that convince you that someone or something bigger than yourself is out there somewhere, and ready to help you out if you ask

for it? No—well, that's okay, because I have a lot
more stories to relate to you.

# CHAPTER SIX

# Try One More Cut Line

This Divine guidance is another incident when listening to that inner voice helped make a last-minute decision that probably saved my life. Even though it seemed like a wrong choice at the time given the situation, and without knowing if it would produce favourable results.

It was in 1986, and perhaps, in late November, Larry called me around 9:30 a.m. to ask if I'd help them track down a bull moose his brother had wounded earlier that morning. They were heading west on Highway 43 from Whitecourt, and just a few miles before the Iosegun River, his brother got out of the truck and had shot at a bull, which was heading into the bush after it had crossed the highway in front of them. Larry still had to deliver his newspapers to Valleyview, Alberta, so he couldn't start tracking it and didn't want to leave his little brother alone in the bush miles from nowhere.

Larry and his brother returned to town and called me, so I drove in to meet them, and we travelled together in their vehicle to the location. They showed me where the bull's tracks entered the bush. The snow was at least 16 inches deep on the ground and some fresh drops of blood on the snow were easy to see. Then both of them continued to Valleyview and would return in about three hours to see if I'd found the animal.

By now, it was around 11 a.m., and it was -15 degrees Celsius (5°F) as I struck off after the bull, and they left to finish their run. As usual, I followed the trail very slowly through the thick bush and expected to see it at any moment. I noticed it had bedded down a couple hundred metres off the highway. There was only a small trace of blood on the snow, and I could not determine if it was seriously injured as the bull had gotten up and walked away.

These clues were significant since it was a good two hours before anyone entered the bush on its trail, and it hadn't left because I spooked it. Therefore, it wasn't hurt that badly, or it would have stayed in its bed and stiffened up. I crossed cut line after cut line following its tracks, and the very faint blood trail got less and less with just a drop every 20–25 metres (22–27 yards). There was no sun to keep track of direction as it was overcast, and by 1 p.m., bad weather was moving in, and it started to snow heavily. I kept on its trail, and the bull didn't stop but didn't run either.

Finally, by around four o'clock, I lost its trail amongst the tracks of several other moose, and there was no blood sign, to distinguish which one I needed to follow. I knew it was late in the day but had forgotten my watch at home, although the continually darkening sky told me it would be dark very soon. Due to the heat from my legs and walking all day in deep snow, my wool pants became caked with crusted snow and ice. It was snowing pretty hard by the time I followed one seismic line to the upper bank of the Iosegun River.

You might think that was a good thing, except for the fact that I thought I was heading in a different direction and wasn't sure this was the Iosegun at all. In short, by the time I discovered I was on a riverbank, I was lost. Considering it might be the Iosegun since I didn't have any aerial photography with me, I wondered how far I was from the highway. Of course, throughout the day, I had been talking to God as there was no one else around, and no one else would have the patience to listen to me for five hours straight anyway.

When I realized I was lost and it was getting dark, I looked around for a spot to build a lean-to and spend the night. I knew I had to start now, or it would be pitch black very soon, and I would have great difficulty getting anything built. The temperature had dropped to around -20 degrees Celsius (-4°F) by then, and the snow had let up a bit, but the north wind was blowing at probably about 30 kilometres per hour (20 mph). Being soaked from the thighs down and having sweated profusely all day, not having a fire would mean they would be searching for a frozen corpse in the morning.

I thought I'd try signaling with my rifle, hoping Larry and his brother would signal back, and I could get a direction as to which way to head. So, I fired off three rounds spaced evenly about four to five seconds apart and waited for a reply, but none came. I tried again a few minutes later with the same results. Now I was a little more worried as I had no direction to head and no idea how far I was from the highway.

With ice covering my pants and my upper body soaked with sweat, it was freezing and cold as the wind continued to pick up. All-day, I had been walking in aspen and poplar stands, with virtually no coniferous timber, which is best for making a shelter in winter. Right near the top of the riverbank, I found a tiny stand of black spruce about 3 metres high (10 feet) and only about 10 metres (11 yards) across, where I thought I could quickly build a makeshift shelter.

I had spent several nights in a lean-to in winter before, but I always had a warm sleeping bag and a good fire. I also wasn't soaking wet from melting snow and sweat, and I knew this was a terrible situation. If I fell asleep, I would succumb to hypothermia long before morning and never wake up.

Just then, I had an inner voice say, *"Just head down this cut line and see if it comes to a road."* I dismissed the thought as I didn't have time to waste if I wanted to stay alive. I had to get a shelter built and start a fire, which would be difficult in the wind, and then I'd have to keep it going all night in the deep snow.

My only other choice, and it was risky, would be to stay on my feet all night. This may seem a little strange to say, but no one has ever frozen to death while standing upright and walking slowly. If you are lost in a snowstorm, and not totally exhausted like I was getting close to, at that point, then walking slowly in a small circle, no more than maybe 6 metres (20 feet) in diameter might keep you alive until morning, if you didn't sit down.

You are accomplishing a few important things in doing that. *First* of all, you have stayed in one area and not struck off in an unknown direction, never to be found again. *Secondly*, you aren't expending much energy, and you aren't sweating, but most importantly, you are keeping blood moving and staying somewhat warm. *Thirdly*, you will stay awake, and I suggest singing or humming songs all night as you move and never sit down. You can walk for 10 to 12 hours if you don't exert yourself, and maybe by then, a search party will be out to locate your remains and will have to settle for you still being alive. This is my own theory, by the way, and thankfully I've never had to put it to the test—but logically, it would be effective.

But before I decided on this action, the feeling persisted that I should walk down the cut line, so I thought—okay, just 15 minutes more, and then I have to stop, no questions asked, and get ready for a very tough night. I walked as fast as I could in the deep snow to cover as much ground as possible and then came to a "Y" in the cut line after about 360 metres (400 yards). I felt I should take the one to the left for some reason and hustled down it and came to an oil wellsite and a snowplowed road. It was glorious to find as the walking would be far easier, but oil field roads go for miles from well to well. And they all look alike, with nothing to distinguish if it is the main road heading out of the area.

I started down the road in the dark, and after about 20 minutes, saw headlights coming my way. I was going to stop this truck if I had to lie on the road—at least I would die warm after he ran over me!

I didn't have to, though, as he pulled up beside me, rolled down his window, and said, *"Are you Merv, your friends are waiting for you?"* It was a Fish and Wildlife officer from Fox Creek. He had stopped by Larry's truck on the highway to find out why they had stopped in the snowstorm, and they told him I was out there somewhere. So, they stayed parked on the road, and he came in looking for me.

If I hadn't listened to that inner voice talking to me and hadn't been on that road, it would have been my last night on this Earth. He drove me to Larry's vehicle, which took nearly 15 minutes because of the convoluted road system. It would have taken me many hours to walk out, and only if I had known which roads to choose. It was interesting that he had worked in the same Fish and Wildlife office I had in Swan River, Manitoba, and we knew the same people, although that had been about nine years earlier. I thanked him and got into Larry's truck.

I told Larry that I tried to signal with my rifle to get a direction, but they must not have been up here by then. They said they had parked on the road and had been there for hours, and had heard me each time I fired a shot.

I was a little puzzled at this and asked why they hadn't signaled back? It was a very desperate situation for me, but Larry said they did. He said he signaled back again with his .22 caliber rifle. Yep, that's right! Larry didn't want to waste three rounds from his .308, so he signaled with a .22 caliber long rifle cartridge. For those non-shooters, the term *long rifle cartridge* is a bit of a misnomer. "The bullet and cartridge are about an inch long and only .22 of an-inch in diameter." A .308 is roughly three inches long, and the casing holds ten times the amount of gun powder as a .22 caliber round. Plus, Larry was miles downwind of me and that .22 caliber round would probably not have been heard at even 300 metres (330 yards) into that wind.

So, in my mind, there was more than one incident of *divine intervention*. If Larry had used the .308, and I had heard it, I would have struck off into the solid bush in that direction to try and make it over five miles in total darkness. I would have gotten hopelessly lost and died of exposure within a few hours. But because I didn't hear him, I listened to the instructions of that inner voice telling me to stay on that cut line and follow it to see if I came to any roads, and I did.

I don't know about you, but to me, that was God or my guardian angel intervening that night to keep me alive. I wasn't mad at Larry, as I knew he was incredibly cheap with his ammunition. I once backed him up when he stalked up on a seven-foot cinnamon-coloured black bear around an old wellsite berm. We suddenly came upon it at around 6.5 metres (7 yards) away. He shot it, and the bear went wild biting at its wound, and I expected a quick follow up shot from his .308 lever action.

However, I watched in disbelief as Larry carefully ejected the empty casing into his hand and put it in his pocket before chambering another round. After the bear spun around twice biting at its wound, it took off running at a right angle from us, and I dropped it with my 6mm Model 600 Remington Mohawk at about 20 metres (22 yards). It could have been on us in less than half that time while Larry collected his empty casing to reload it later.

Everyone has their priorities, although I never trusted myself to track wounded animals all on my own for them, ever again. My life was worth more than the cost of three rounds from a .308 to my wife and kids.

But the fact that Larry used the .22 caliber instead prevented me from getting lost that night and trying to make it through to him in dense bush in the dark. So, he did what God wanted him to do.

# CHAPTER SEVEN

# They Stayed Calm

On the advice of my dear wife, who was editing this book and subjected to reading the following story, she has *advised* that no one should read what's coming up while eating, if they have a weak stomach or a vivid imagination. I guess that's because I gave it to her to read while she was having breakfast. My bad, but at my age, you got to have a little fun, right! I'll give you another warning just before the part she found disturbing.

~~~~~~

I had another experience while I was still a Forest Officer in Whitecourt in 1982, where I believe *divine intervention* guided me in a manner that possibly spared me from something severe occurring. On a couple of different occasions, I could have landed on a slab in the morgue or, at the very least, put me in the hospital. The following pages describe the conditions I was working in to give you a realistic feel for the environment. Read at your own risk, or skip to the next story. I'm not kidding!

During one particularly bad fire season in the mid-80s, I was exported for fire action into Northern Alberta on the Haig Lake fire, which was 168,000 hectares (415,137 acres) in size. I was assigned to be the sector boss on a 54-kilometre (34-mile) stretch of fire line with three D-8 cat bulldozers and four 28-man native fire crews, stationed in camps along the fire line as well as three helicopters at my disposal. It was a relatively small sector and fairly quiet by then, as there was a total of 32 fire crews, 24 cats, 21 light helicopters, and 12 mediums of the Bell 204 size and up to the twin-engine 212 in size; all bucketing the fire line in more active sections. There were also three water bomber groups that would be called in from the Town of Peace River to handle any massive flare-ups.

My job was to keep the crews working in my sector and put out hot spots that threatened to jump the fire line that had been cut out by the bulldozers. My day started at 5 a.m. when my 206 Jet Ranger helicopter arrived from the base-camp to pick me up to scout the line for hot spots and to visit the other crews at their camps. The firefighters would then get up and have breakfast before heading out along the line in their section.

In the middle of summer in the far north of Alberta, the sun didn't set until after midnight, and my day would end around 11 p.m. when I'd get dropped off at my tent camp location. I would be dropped off by my second helicopter, as they had maximum flight times of ten hours per day for pilots, and I was burning up flight times for two pilots with around 18 hours a day of helicopter time. They would return to the comfort of the main firebase staging area, about 24 kilometres (15 miles) across-country for some well-deserved rest and good meals and a shower. No such luxuries were available in the bush tent camps. I'd go like that for 21 days straight before getting two days off and starting over again.

In case you think that working on a remote wildfire would be a hoot, and would like to have been there, I need to say that it wasn't luxury living and fine dining during those 21 days. On occasion, I had to unroll my sleeping bag in that 12x14 foot, orange plastic wall tent that had eight native smokers in it, all sleeping on the lumpy ground covered with a sheet of plastic. After spending all day choking on smoke from the fire line, they had to relax by sucking in smoke from a cigarette, before sleeping. Yeah, I know! I don't understand it either, but then again, I'm not a smoker. And if you don't think white people experience discrimination, then you haven't been the only white authority in a remote camp of natives for weeks on end.

On other occasions, I was alone in my tent, which I preferred, but they would always manage to erect my tent next to the meat pit. I assumed they were hoping that my screams would alert the rest of the camp to the fact that there was a bear in camp. Sometimes they'd get creative and stretch the plastic sheet I was sleeping on, to the outside of the tent walls about 30 centimetres (12 inches) or more, and then drape it over a log lying on the ground on either side of the tent. That way, when it rained, all the water running off the roof would run down the walls and onto the plastic sheet. You guessed it, and then the water would be directed right into the tent and soak all my belongings, including my sleeping bag—all kinds of fun, eh!

Meals were often sketchy; the native cooks would merely boil tender A-1 cuts of sirloin beef steak in a couple big 30-litre (6.5 imperial gallons) pots to save time. Do you have any idea what top-quality steak is like after boiling for an hour in a large kettle, along with 30 more of them in there? No spices, and as rubbery and tough as the soles on our boots.

> *Now here's the part that you might want to avoid reading while eating!*

And the garbage barrel always ended up being near my end of the table for some reason, as that was the only spot left to sit. Then picture 25-plus guys at the table made of rough logs, including the benches, with lots of leftovers each day. The leftover food would all go into an open barrel, placed no more than three feet from my plate, and the volume in the barrel increased over time. Did I say we had flies? No! Well, we had flies and loads of them? The evidence to that was revealed, in that, the barrel—was alive with tens of thousands of maggots writhing all over the rotting meat. When it got overly full, with the maggots falling off in large clumps and splashing on the ground by my feet, they'd finally dump the barrel and start over. That was a day for celebration! Are you hungry yet?

I think I mentioned in the past, or I guess in my second book: '*If Divine Intervention is Real, Do Hunters Experience It?*' that I have an incredible sense of smell. I've never bothered to have this tested, but without a doubt, I have a sense of smell far beyond anyone I know personally, so claiming that I have *hyperosmia* isn't a stretch.

So, put yourself in this situation with three to five days-worth of rotting food in the open air right near your plate. I was sitting with 25 unwashed firefighters, as we had no showers or creeks or any lake nearby. I had just one change of clothes in 21 days myself—and they had one pair of orange coveralls for 21 days, and I wished I couldn't smell anything, but wasn't that lucky. Are you still interested in having the experience?

If you've ever been in a locker room after a sports game, you have a little understanding. But multiply that by 25 people with no baths or washed clothes for anyone over 21 days, and then throw in the rotting food and maggots to cap it off. That's why the flies preferred the rotten meat and mostly left us alone, as we'd probably gag a maggot if it got too close to us.

Oh, and I was usually fortunate that they dug the hole for the camp toilet close to my tent, so I didn't have far to go, I suppose. How thoughtful—right! It was a wondrous thing and a genius of design. It consisted of a pine or spruce log, about six inches in diameter, without the bark removed—there was no sliding around on that thing I guarantee you—unless it was slippery, and that's another issue as to why. The log was nailed horizontally across two trees, about two feet off the ground to serve as the seat which you hungover and tried not to fall over backward as that experience would stick with you for a lifetime. And of course, everyone in the camp used the same toilet log, but they didn't use it very well. And you had to watch where you put your feet as not everyone was able to hit the very shallow hole in the ground.

Think of what that was like, as people would often get diarrhea from the unsanitary food preparation, and one toilet served the camp for 21 days. In case you haven't figured it out, there were no walls and no roof—just the log and the hole and copious contributions by everyone. But to their credit when a new crew arrived, they'd dig another hole a few feet further away and start over. Fortunately, with the sleep deprivation of only roughly four hours per night, even I didn't care, after the first week.

You had to test the sturdiness of that log once in a while before you settled down. It was a great joke for some of the crew to pull the nails most of the way out, which were holding the log in place, so that when a person put their full weight on it as they stretched out over the hole in the ground—well you get the idea! But that never happened until after at least a week of use; otherwise, the gift awaiting the unsuspecting when they hit the hole wasn't as substantial, and the hilarity wasn't as satisfying. As the only white guy in the camp and the Forest Officer, I had to be doubly aware of their need for frivolity to break their boredom. Of course, these conditions are mild compared to third world toiletry and sanitary conditions such as one might find in India, but it was still a little rustic for the 80s in Canada.

*Okay, the disturbing images are over—you're safe to read the rest, according to my beloved editor—but I know you couldn't resist reading it anyway—right!*

On this particular fire, they had a lot of problems with bears as hundreds of them had been forced to the outskirts of the extensive burned-out area by the approaching fire. And of course, that's where all the fire camps, food caches, and garbage pits are located. In a total wilderness area, bears don't know what a human is and are not afraid of them at all.

On more than one occasion, we had to hover low over a black bear or grizzly in the helicopters to scare it off, so the crew boss, who was walking the fire line to check for hot spots, could come down out of the trees and we'd pick him up. They were also fond of the fire hoses that were often strung out well over a mile between relay points where a tank would get filled, and pumps and more hoses went from there further along to the fire line. This method was used because available water was hard to come by, and a set of fire pumps in tandem or even triple could only push the water so far with sufficient pressure due to friction in the hose.

The hoses would vibrate when under high pressure, and the bears walking the cat guard would step on them and feel the vibration. They then liked to bite them and discovered it provided a pleasant cold drink in a *self-serve fountain* kind of way, meaning we had to continually replace the hoses when the water pressure suddenly dropped off. Some bears liked to follow the hose to the end of it, which always caused great excitement for whichever firefighters were using the nozzle.

A helicopter pilot showed me a picture of a 3-metre (9-foot) grizzly standing on hind legs with the nozzle of the fire hose in its mouth, and a 15-metre (50-foot) stream of water spraying out from it. Just trying to do his part, I guess, in fire suppression! And they say that *Smoky the Bear* wasn't real! Yeah, right, we have evidence that he was!

I had heard of the problems and bear attacks they were having before I was even exported to the fire and asked my Chief Forest Officer Ed D. if I should take a rifle. "No, you don't need it," he spouted. "They have a bear shooter that they fly from camp to camp." Right, so if a bear harassed me or the camp, help is only a helicopter's ride away, during daylight only, and maybe a day or two hence for him to get there, as he's busy at other camps! Typical thinking of management who don't have to be in the field, and indeed Ed D. had never been on any large fire camps and had progressed up through the ranks by basically being the only guy around at the time, by his own admission.

At one point, the black bears started to move into our camp as I heard shouting by one of the cooks when she was heading to the meat pit. Oh yeah—I should explain. Up North, the ground at about 2 metres (7 feet) below the surface was always around 10 degrees Celsius (52°F), so digging a hole and covering it was the only cooler we had to keep meat somewhat fresh. As the bear was helping itself, the young warriors grabbed their Pulaski's and charged it, chasing it away. A half an hour later it was back, with the same result, but it didn't run as far. The third time, it just stood up and waited for them, and that was the end of the exercise in bluffing a 180 kilogram

(400-pound) black bear that hadn't been hurt by these humans and had staked a *claim* that the meat pit was his.

I called for the bear shooter and wished I hadn't after he was there for one night. The guy was one of those 50-plus-year-old characters who talked incessantly and laughed at his own jokes and kept ongoing. To make it worse, he slept during the day and was up all night, chattering away in my tent, and my four hours of sleep never happened. He shot a bear in the morning two days later, and thankfully the 204-helicopter arrived with a resupply of fresh food and took it away to end my torment—oh, and they took the bear away as well.

But a few days later, more bears were back in camp, and one of my pilots relayed this to the main firebase camp, which was 24 kilometres (15 miles) away by air. They contacted me, and I confirmed we had a problem, but I didn't want the shooter back as I was tired enough without having to stay awake for 40 hours at a stretch. Then the low cloud ceiling rolled in, and there was heavy ground fog as well, so no helicopters were allowed to fly, and we couldn't get resupplied. The fire crews still went to work and walked out on the fire line, but the female cooks were terrified to stay in camp by themselves, and I can't blame them.

So, I stayed with them and was able to keep them safe during the day, I guess, by being the sacrificial offering if a bear got aggressive. Inwardly, I was angry at my non-hunter, non-shooter chief ranger desk jockey, back in Whitecourt, for not allowing me to take a rifle to camp. When the firefighters returned, the meals were from all canned foods as the bears left nothing fresh behind. The next day, after the firefighting crews left for the day, we had five adult black bears in camp during the middle of the day, and I was as close as 1 metre (3 feet) from some of them, and they weren't budging. They were incredibly *calm*, which was very strange as there had been attacks at other camps with people seriously injured.

I have to admit that I had no idea at the time why they reacted this way other than—*something* was keeping them calm. At any rate, they cleaned out all the food in the camp, and I mean everything except for a few cans here and there, and all we could do was stand back and watch. I even had one come to the open front of my tent and was just a little over a metre (four feet) from me, then turned and slowly walked away as if I wasn't even there, or maybe it was my smell that turned him off, as they can only stomach so much, and I couldn't blame him.

I had two immediate concerns. One was the fact that we had no food for 28 people, 29, including me. The other was that when the bears come back, and with no food left, there would also be a bunch of young, frightened firefighters that may not remain as calm as they should. As a result, the bears might try a fresh sample to see how it tastes. Of course, if we went without food long enough, the frustration in camp could mean that the only white meat there might look tasty as well, or as a sacrifice to the bears, so it was time to do something about it.

As such, I gave in, and late that afternoon just at dusk, I gathered up some fresh D-cell batteries and replaced all eight in one of the handheld radios, which weighed around 2.7 kilograms (6 pounds) at the time, and went to make a call. It was an *eerie* feeling as I was walking uphill a few hundred yards in the very dense fog, and standing on the top of the dirt pile fire line guard pushed up by a bulldozer. I held the radio up over my head with one hand, so the little 45-centimetre (18-inch) antenna was as high as possible and held the mic in the other hand, as they had a separate mic on a coiled cord. I then tried to call the base camp.

It was an extreme range at 24 kilometres (15 miles) for one of those radios, and my communication was all broken up, but the whole Fire

Control office staff at the firebase heard it—as relayed to me afterward. It went something like this, *"five bears...all...food-gone...camp...cooks afraid...injuries...shooter."* That broken up dialogue was a little worrying to the command team at the firebase, and shortly most of the 150-plus people there at the camp were aware of the situation. "They," on the other hand, were living in the relative lap of luxury, with about 25 Atco oil rig trailers. They had all the amenities, showers, bathrooms, and a huge mess hall with several cooks and large walk-in coolers operating on substantial diesel generators to keep everything fresh.

I never got much of a reply, just static and only a word or two, *"can't fly...grounded...might replace...morning."* From that brief snippet, I took it that since my 21 days were up tomorrow, they were replacing me, if they could get to us. So, the boys stayed up all night by the fire with axes and Pulaski's in hand, and I had a good night's sleep, snuggled up next to my fire axe. At around 9:30 a.m., a black ERA Alaskan helicopter flew in.

A pair of x-Vietnam pilots flew the helicopter. They flew on the deck along the rivers and lakes to the cut line that headed our way from the east; then travelled another 4.8 kilometres (3 miles) up to our camp along the cut line right at treetop level as the fog was still really dense. The bear shooter and my replacement jumped out, along with about 20 cases of food that the fire crew was quick to unload. I then jumped in with little more than a smile and a wave goodbye to my replacement and a warning to wear earplugs if he wanted to sleep at all.

So, you may not think it was much in the way of *divine intervention* if you are used to walking among very wild adult black bears that were displaced, competitive for food, and hungry. But having five adult black bears not accustomed to humans, like park bears would be, wandering the tent camp for several hours was a bit unnerving. Coming within arms-reach of us, primarily me, as the cooks hid in their tent, without a single person injured, seemed surreal. But I guess you had to have been there to understand that it certainly felt like something extraordinary was at work, to keep it from all going terribly wrong. Thoughts of "Daniel in the Lion's Den" came to mind at the time, although I was there by choice, and all I could do was shake my head and marvel at the experience.

I suppose if God wanted me to have this experience and learn to trust in a situation like this, then not bringing my 7mm Magnum rifle was a must. Otherwise, I would have handled the bear incursions all on my own and never had this unique experience to remember. So, looking back, should I be angry with my Chief Ranger for something that perhaps God intended to happen? Obviously not!

# CHAPTER EIGHT

# I Turned My Back

The threat for one's safety wasn't only from bears on the fire line, or helicopter accidents, or personal injury, sometimes the people were a threat as well. On one occasion on the same fire, I had a particularly challenging crew working further down the line. As I would fly the fire line moving more hoses or pumps to other locations, I would see them all jump up in the distance and start shovelling and chopping like mad when they heard the helicopter approaching. Then as I looked back after we flew by, they'd all put their tools down and would sit on the ground and chat. I was a little annoyed at their work ethics as I was getting a lot of pressure from the firebase that not enough progress was happening in my sector, and I knew why.

I don't begrudge anyone from taking a break once in a while, as you can see, the working and living conditions were less than ideal. However, getting paid for 14- to 16-hour days while they put in maybe one to two hours of actual work, and I took the flak for it, wasn't going to continue. I guess what annoyed me the most is that they thought I was too dumb to realize what they were doing.

Now before anyone mistakenly gets the impression that I am racist, since I was dealing with native firefighters, referred to as First Nations people, their race has absolutely nothing to do with it. The character of an individual makes all the difference, not their ethnic background or colour of their skin.

In these situations, it is the integrity of the crew boss. If he is lazy and conniving, the rest of the crew has little choice but to go along with what he says, or they'll have a very rough time in camp, and it doesn't matter what the ethnic background is. On more than one occasion, we had to airlift one or two guys out of a camp for medical aid because they had run afoul of someone else on the crew, and no one was talking.

Also, fire crews from particular reserves had a bad reputation, primarily because their crew bosses did. The firefighting crews from First Nations reserves in the Rocky Mountain

House area of Alberta were people of exceptional character, and excellent people to work with, and also to spend time with, within the camp. Whereas some fire crews from the northeast part of the province, south of Fort McMurray had the opposite reputation, and I had one of those on this occasion.

The fact that one Forest Officer reported when a new crew came in to replace a previous one from this particular reserve, on his sector, they refused to use the camp location and insisted that it be moved. The reason was that they said the departing crew had defecated in every tent in the camp before they were airlifted back to base after their 21 days on the fire line. They did this despicable act because they had heard which reserve the replacement crews were coming from, and they didn't get along. Good character knows no ethnic boundary, and neither does a rotten one.

So on one day, as I flew over and witnessed the same repeat performance, I had the helicopter put me down 1.6 kilometres (1 mile) away, and I walked up the cat guard to where the crew was, which was all sitting around in a group at two o'clock in the afternoon. I never announced myself, but I just stood there, back in the trees a few metres, and watching them, but not hidden. I was there for probably 15 minutes before one of them noticed me, not even 8 metres (26 feet) away from him, and the reaction was like insects scattering when the light turns on, with the addition of a barrage of expletives, mostly in Cree. They were grabbing their tools and running in every direction, and I caught the eye of the crew boss and waved him over. I told him I was docking everyone's pay today to only half a day. I then turned around and walked off and used my radio to call for the helicopter to pick me up further up the line.

I imagine the crew wasn't happy with me, and probably not pleased with the crew boss either. A few days later, as I flew over them again, I found one squad standing around doing nothing, while one guy was chopping at the base of a tall standing spruce tree, which was not on fire. I immediately knew what they were doing. It was a chopping competition to see who could fell a tree in the shortest amount of time. I turned to the pilot and shook my head and said, "This crap has gotta stop, and I'm ending it now."

I had the helicopter land within 32 metres (35 yards) of them, right on a wider part of the cat guard, with the machine facing them. The pilot looked a little nervous and said into the mic, "Do you want me to come with you for backup?"

I said, "No, I'll be fine. You wait right here." I exited the Jet Ranger and walked towards the group with my least happy expression.

I asked what they were doing. And the same crew boss who was with this squad of seven said there was smoke coming from the top, so they had to cut it down—along with the other three trees that were also on the ground already. Okay, I'm a Forest Officer who works on wildfires, among other duties, and I'm pretty good at *cold trailing*. That was "the practice, believe it or not, of putting your hands into every nook and cranny in the ground in a burnt over area, to make sure there is no heat there, and an underground fire wasn't still burning." This method was used before we had the handheld laser heat-sensing devices that would do that for you today, and keep you from burning your hands.

I said to the crew boss and squad, "Let's go have a look," and they followed me as I walked over to the top of the tree and felt it. Of course, it had been out for over a month, and I asked them if they thought I was stupid. I didn't wait for an answer!

I squared off with the group and said, "I've had enough of this crap." And I told them they weren't getting paid for today and to return to camp as I was firing the entire crew. With all of them standing in front of me, shouting curses at me, and two of them raising their axes towards me, while they spit on my uniform, I turned around with my *back to them* and just stood there. At this point, I was quite puzzled as to why I didn't immediately walk to the helicopter as I stayed there for probably 30 seconds. I then started walking back to the machine and noticed the pilot's eyes seemed to be as "large as golf balls." I was tempted to look behind me, but I didn't.

I got in the machine and buckled up as he shook his head and grinned, saying, "That was tense! You're lucky you didn't get an axe in the back because a couple of them were tempted, and it looked like they were discussing it."

I just nodded and said, "Let's go." You might think I was a seasoned old veteran and knew what I was doing out there, laying down the law for a group of natives, when in fact, I was only 25 years old at the time and didn't have much of a clue.

I had to provide a report the next day to the firebase why I was firing the crew. I explained the whole scenario to the chief fire boss, who was twice my age. He sat back and grinned as he shook his head and said, "I don't know how you did that, but it was the only thing that probably kept you from being axed."

He told me that while they were issuing the cheques to the crew before being flown out, they had discovered that the crew boss had just been let out on bail and was awaiting trial for murder before he came out to the fire line. He was known for having a big ego and a hot temper. Being embarrassed in front of the other young natives like that would normally have caused him to physically assault me at the very least, and at worst, plant an axe in my back.

But in the native culture, after an elder or person of authority or the entire tribe, chastises one of their own for bad behaviour, *they turn their backs to them and stand there.* It's a form of banishing them due to the shame and disrespect they have brought by their actions. He told me that that one act probably saved my life, as I was addressing them in the way their people would, for showing such disrespect.

He said if I had continued to challenge him, he would have had to act to save face. If I had run, he probably would have acted out his anger by chasing me down, and the rest would have joined in with him. It may have turned out badly for the pilot as well since eyewitnesses are a terrible thing. Then, I understood why the pilot looked so alarmed.

I also now knew precisely why I had suddenly turned my back to them and stood there for so long. And believe me, 30 seconds is a very long time when you have eight guys close enough to spit on your uniform, shouting curses at you, and carrying axes; and in the eyes of the helicopter pilot, raising them to strike me down.

To me, since I knew nothing about this particular reaction in their culture, the fact that I did it without planning it, was the result of *divine intervention*. You can make up your own mind.

I have the suspicion that some of us don't keep the same guardian angel for all of our lifetimes. I suspect that mine has taken stress leave or felt a need to be replaced on occasion, what do you think?

# CHAPTER NINE

# If You Have Integrity

So, you might be wondering if *divine intervention* is always there to give you a hand at bettering yourself economically or by being successful in other areas of life. As you will note in my second book involving hunting stories, you are partially right. Still, there is another aspect whereby you receive absolutely no personal benefit. Yet, compelled to act because you have integrity, and if you did nothing, it would haunt you for a very long time.

Acting out of a sense of conscience to do the right thing, despite the cost to yourself, seems to be a difficult thing for people to undertake these days. Political events all over the world would testify to that, but especially in Canada and the USA throughout 2019. Being privy to details that expose wrongdoing and your reaction to it is also an act of *divine intervention*. It places you in a position to choose to put your integrity ahead of personal benefit and do what's right, or you will ignore the facts and turn a blind eye to it all, just because you don't like the source of information? Your answer will define where you are in a relationship with God and with your personal sense of morality.

If you have no relationship with either one, then your choice is simple. Just keep your head down, do as you're told, and you will be better off, as long as you can justify what you have seen or learned with your convictions. You will have preserved your favoured status, but you have lost all integrity. You will also be responsible for all the harm that ensues by your inaction and unwillingness to stand up for what is right and to expose what is wrong. The term *hypocrite* would suffice, but there are more persuasive words that can also apply.

There are times in our lives when we are put into a situation, not of our choosing, and yet our actions will make a significant difference if we dare to do the right thing. Do you have the courage to do the right thing, if faced with the choice put before you, through *divine intervention*? Only you can answer that, but you will also answer for that choice you make when you meet the one who asks you why you made the choice that you did.

I have two stories I will share on this subject, and you can judge for yourself if what I did was right or wrong, based on your own sense of morality and how you might have responded in these situations. Of course, your judgement of my actions won't affect me; it will merely reveal who you are.

# CHAPTER TEN

# Couldn't Bury It

In about 1983, I was a fire boss on a 120-hectare (296-acre) forest fire that had mostly burned itself out—located about 32 kilometres (20 miles) north of the Eagle Forestry Tower, which is roughly an hour's drive west and slightly north of the town of Whitecourt, Alberta. There had been three crews on the fire for the past three or four weeks. It had been pretty much suppressed, and they were in the mop-up phase. A dry lightning storm had just passed through this part of Alberta, and the next day there were another 140 new fires to contend with, so they were pulling crews off of fires that were already under control, to man-up at new firebases further north.

The day I arrived at the fire camp for the Eagle Tower fire, busses were leaving with the crews that headed to the Swan Hills' fires. One new squad arrived, and I was there with eight firefighters and one cook, to monitor the fire line and ensure it didn't cross the cat guard that had encircled it. It seemed like a reasonably cushy job at this point as all I had to do was fly the fire line each morning with a helicopter and an infrared heat detector to look for hot spots, and send the squad out to take care of any that flared up. Then on the second day there, something was dropped in my lap that I hadn't expected.

I had just gotten back from being out on the fire line all afternoon and discovered that a five-ton truck had shown up when I was away. It had unloaded a one-week supply of fresh meat, produce, and canned foods for three crews of firefighters; that's 84 men, including a few women as cooks. The food order for these items was placed the day before the crews were to be shipped out, and it was no longer required, but no one had cancelled the food order. It was between $9,000 and $10,000 worth of food in mid-80s dollars, and I only had a total of ten people to feed, including myself. All this food would go to waste if I didn't find some use for it right away.

I contacted my Forestry Headquarters and talked to the fire chief on duty and explained the mistake. I asked if they could send a truck, and we'd load it up and send it after the crews that went to the Swan Hills' fires.

Their response floored me! He said, "You still have a couple of D8 cats on the fire, don't you?"

"Yes," I responded.

"Well, just bury it all then."

I said, "Bury it; we shouldn't be wasting it like that, should we?" To which he replied that they had already placed the food orders for the new fire camps, and they do this all the time.

I asked, "What do you mean you do this all the time?"

And he, being a 20-year veteran of the Forest Service, said, "We always bury everything leftover from fires and order new stuff. From plastic fire crew tents to sleeping bags and even cooking utensils, but especially all the leftover food. It's no big deal, get it done."

If you've read more about my upbringing in my second book on *divine intervention*, you might understand how this would bother me. Throwing away perfectly good food was just something I would never do, having been hungry so many times in my early years. There were too many people struggling these days, as Alberta was going through an economic downturn, and here I was supposed to bury $10,000 worth of fresh food, and I felt sick. What bothered me

more, though, was the fact that my fellow officers did this all the time. Blatant disregard for
taxpayer's dollars was hard to digest in the moment, let alone the waste and on top of that the
pollution.

It was ironic that as a Forest Officer, I had
the capability and responsibility to ticket anyone
I found, leaving refuse in the forest. That means
any garbage either on the surface or buried. My
fellow officers, charged with upholding the Forest Act, and all its regulations were engaged in
blatant pollution of the environment on a regular
basis, and they thought nothing of it while penal-
izing the public for infractions far minor to this.

They were doing this not only with the full
knowledge of the forest superintendents across
the province, but on the direct orders from them
because it was more convenient, and it kept their
budget demands up. I was a relatively new Forest
Officer only having joined in 1981, and I just
hadn't come across this yet—to be faced with the
choice I now had to make.

I could follow orders and waste the food, in
full sight of the other firefighters, and demonstrate what a *hypocrite* I was as a Forest Officer,
and feel sick about it all at the same time. Or find
another way of dealing with it. So, I prayed about
it, and the thought came to me to talk to the cat
operator before he left for the day to return home.

It turned out he was also the owner of the two D8 cats on-site, and I went up to him and explained the dilemma, and he said, *"Yeah, we can bury it,"* but not in a very enthusiastic tone. I assumed he had to do this on other occasions, and it probably didn't sit well with him either. You did what they told you to do as a contractor, or you would be dismissed from the fire, and your name was taken off the list of companies to contact.

I then asked if he had any trucks he could bring up, and a smile crossed his face as he replied, *"I sure do."* He also said they have some big walk-in coolers in Blue Ridge, the little hamlet just 22.5 kilometres (14 miles) east of Whitecourt that was quite a depressed area economically, with a lot of dilapidated homes still occupied.

I told him we couldn't personally benefit from this, so he was to haul the food down there and put it in the coolers and then invite the town folk to help themselves. He was very enthusiastic about helping, and of course, this wouldn't be on him, it would be on me, as it was by my order. The trucks arrived the next morning, and all the extra food was loaded and removed, and he did just as we had planned. He had gone to the poorest sections of the small village, which is most of it, and spread the word, and the food got utilized instead of wasted. By doing this, I didn't have to violate our regulations of the Provincial Forest Act, and I was a happy camper until I got back, that is.

Four days later, they manned down the fire, and everyone returned home since we hadn't seen any hot spots for a couple of days after it rained through the area. As I walked into the forestry warehouse in Whitecourt, the warehouse manager nicknamed Rocky, a cantankerous old codger, laid the law down to me as soon as he saw me come in. He said, "You'd better take a seat," which I did on one of the chairs across from his desk, and I asked what's up. He said, "You've done it this time. Your career is over." I didn't know how to take him as he often used bluster to get a reaction, but he assured me he was dead serious.

The Forest Superintendent Cliff H. had got wind of what I had done, via another forest officer who had been made aware of it in Blue Ridge, when one of the town's folk thanked him for doing this. Funny though, he took the credit and the appreciation for supplying the food, then he ran to management to tattle like a good little boy. Ah, well, such will be the integrity of public servants who look after themselves at the expense of others.

Rocky said that Cliff H. wanted me in his office as soon as I got back, and I was going to understand how serious this was. I'd be lucky to keep my job, but most assuredly, I'd be demoted at the very least and perhaps transferred out to another forest district.

I said, "For what, giving away food that was going to get wasted anyway?"

He said, "For violating a direct order to bury it, and for acting without the authorization."

Then I said, "Well, I asked if there was another solution that wouldn't waste it and they wouldn't provide one, and since what I did wouldn't have been authorized anyway, as the Forest Service just wants to waste it, then doing it was the only thing I could come up with."

He said, "None of that matters, you've screwed your career, and now you'll pay for it!"

At this point, I became angry, and I mean furious. I stood up and came up to Rocky's desk. I said, "Really? How would the Forest Service like to have the local newspaper find out that it buries tens of thousands of dollars of food and materials after every forest fire camp once manned down?" And, "That we violate the Forest Act, we are sworn to uphold, every time we bury canned goods and plastics in the crown forests to hide our laziness, in taking it all back out again. Then we ticket and fine the public when we see them leave an empty can of beans on the ground or a plastic bag?"

Rocky was quiet this whole time, but his eyes were getting wider. I then added, "I have a good friend who is a government social worker in Whitecourt and manages the food bank for people having a hard time right now. How do you think David N. is going to react when he finds out that another segment of the government is wasting thousands of dollars of food when they are pleading for donations?"

There was still no response from Rocky, as he could see I was visibly distraught at these threats, and I was shaking in anger. I then concluded with, "I'm heading to my office right now, and you can call Cliff and tell him I'll be there in half an hour, if he wants to go this route, I'll be waiting for his call!" and I left.

I went to my office, expecting the worst, and nothing happened. My Chief Ranger Ed D., who has never stood up for anyone ever in his life, didn't say a word to me and didn't make eye contact, either? I also didn't get a telephone call from upstairs, which was headquarters for the Whitecourt Forest, and where Cliff H's office was.

Was I scared, yeah, you bet I was? I had a wife and two little children at home, one of them very sick with a heart problem, and I had a 19 percent mortgage on my used house trailer. Who wouldn't be afraid? I had to trust God now as there wasn't a single person at work that would stand up for me, and that's the sad part. Working with people you looked up to and realizing that they had no integrity, no backbone, and would choose to protect themselves and violate their own rules rather than doing what was right, was a sickening feeling, but that's government, I guess.

But three days later, a new policy was passed down from the Provincial Headquarters in Edmonton, right from the Deputy Minister of Forests. It stated, "All leftover foodstuffs and usable material are to be recovered from forest fires and returned to the regional warehouses to be distributed to food banks and social services." I was stunned! It seemed that Cliff H. was the author of the new legislation and had convinced Provincial Headquarters that it would be in the best interest of public relations to undertake this change in policy.

No one said a word to me, and I was smart enough not to utter a word either, as gloating about this wouldn't have been a brilliant move. However, my actions were not appreciated by management or the other forest officers, because now they had more work to do after a fire, and the food had to be brought back to Regional Headquarters and stored until distributed, instead of buried. I wondered if there was guilt attached to their anger towards me, as it revealed how spineless and disingenuous, they were in not carrying out their duties to protect the environment while punishing the public?

Then again, I was always on the outside of the group since I didn't go drinking every Friday night with them, and didn't act anything like them since I was deemed a religious nut. Even though I never preached to anyone, I wouldn't back down when harassed about my faith either.

Sometimes you need to get angry, even as a Christian, or a faithful believer in any religion if you have to stand up to something that's morally or ethically wrong. Or you can go with the flow, keep your head down and take care of yourself, remaining in good favour with authority. Unfortunately, those people don't realize that backbones are grown and not bought!

There was another related incident a year later involving 21 barrels of avgas. The barrels stored at the warehouse yard supplied the fueling of a local Robinson R22 helicopter that Cliff H. would use to tour the fire areas. The fire season was over, and the avgas remained, which was 100- to 130-octane and leaded fuel. Leaded gas never degrades, even after years in storage. But if there were a surplus, an explanation would be necessary for why there was an excess. And on top of that, there wouldn't be money in the fire budget to buy more next year.

Rocky and Cliff H. made arrangements to get one of our initial attack crew foremen to load up all the barrels and dump them in the forest somewhere, where no one would find out. With specific instructions to the guy to not tell me! I know that because I questioned the initial attack foreman a few times to find out where they dumped it, and he wouldn't tell me.

He was a favourite of Cliff H. after that and groomed to go to Forestry School and become a forest ranger at Cliff's urging. His name was Dan, and he was taking his commercial flight training on twin engines aircraft at the White-court Flying School. He was a likable guy who had asked me many questions about God and my faith in the past. But when it came to where his "bread was buttered," he knew how to keep his mouth shut, even though the most toxic fuel we possessed had just been intentionally dumped somewhere in the Whitecourt Forest.

I was angry, but I now had no evidence and no place to sample so I could do nothing. Are you wondering if Dan became a Forest Officer, groomed by Cliff H.?

What happened shortly after—was quite sad. One weekend, when Dan was with his girl-friend at the bunkhouse on the warehouse grounds, a kid on a Honda trike was running around on the warehouse property. So, Dan took one of the forestry's Honda trikes and chased him. But Dan had his girlfriend sitting behind him on the trike, and as he went over a bump, she bounced off and suffered spinal injuries and was severely injured. They responded quickly and got her to the hospital, but she died only hours later.

I felt so bad for Dan, and Cliff H. had no choice but to fire him. Last I heard was that Dan was driving a taxi in Calgary. So much promise for a young man, but when you decide to do things you know are wrong, often things don't work out as planned. I'm sure Cliff H. felt terrible too, but also probably hoped that Dan wouldn't reveal anything about secretly dumping the avgas for him on crown land, which would have ended his career.

# CHAPTER ELEVEN

# I Am Terrified, But How Do I Do This?

I had many small encounters that set me at odds with forest management over the intervening years. I always seemed to be in the wrong place at the right time to witness them doing things they had explicitly ordered everyone else not to do, and knowing that I caught them at it, was a thorn in their side.

But the next major incident occurred in the fall of 1988 and was far more unnerving for me than the first time I crossed management. I had got to know the head of another government department in Whitecourt, and I guess he knew me quite well, in that I would do the right thing regardless of the cost. That's not a typical government employee trait; by the way. You will never be asked that question at an interview.

I won't use his real name, but let's call him Bob since he has gone on to have a long and successful career in government, right up to the highest levels of upper management. Even though I believe he might be retired now, I wouldn't want to cause him any stress. He called me one day to come to his office and told me that there was something about to happen that they could do nothing about, and it wasn't right.

On arriving there, he took me into his office and closed the door. I was wondering at that moment if I was in trouble in some way. I was searching my mind for potential misdeeds that might account for this kind of privacy, from a friend in authority. It turned out that it had nothing to do with me at all on the surface. It involved a permit his office had received regarding the bleach kraft pulp mill in Hinton, Alberta, which had recently been bought by Weldwood from St. Regis Pulp and Paper in 1986.

As part of their restructuring plan, they wanted to expand their caustic soda settling ponds to be able to increase the size of the mill. They had at least two settling ponds at the time, which held roughly 450,000 cubic yards each of the most caustic effluent imagined. By the way, that's roughly 914,442 tons combined. Nothing lived if it accidentally fell into those ponds. I asked Bob how they could do that since it was a total violation of the Environmental Act and everything that Alberta Environment stood for on behalf of the people of the province.

Bob said that Weldwood had gotten permission from the Department of Environment to drain the ponds into the Athabasca River at 3 a.m. on a Sunday on a particular date, which I can no longer remember. Still, it was in late September or early October, and just a week or so away.

If you're curious how many imperial gallons, that is, it's 90,900,000 per settling pond or 181,800,000 imperial gallons in total. If that number doesn't impress you, we can look at it in litres since I'm in Canada. That effluent comes to 687,600,000 litres of toxic, caustic soda that the Alberta Environment was going to allow Weldwood to dump into the pristine Athabasca River because it was cheaper. Think about that for a moment and realize that this goes on all the time between government and industry. For the sake of cutting costs and maintaining profit levels for shareholders in many sectors, but primarily forestry, oil and gas, and mining, and only this one time—it was caught before it happened.

The Athabasca River was a very clean river at that point as it was coming from the Rocky Mountains through Jasper National Park and about as pristine as one could ever hope a water-way could be.

Their thinking was that no one would be up at that time of the morning, and by the time it was light, the effluent and thousands of dead fish would be many kilometres downstream, and no one would notice. There wasn't another commu-nity that would observe the river for 212 kilometres (132 miles) downstream, and that would be Whitecourt. And yet the river ran along the north side of town; there were no dwellings or businesses along the river's edge, so perhaps not even then would it be noticed and certainly not if it passed in the night when the effluent got there.

The river was also added to by many tribu-taries along the way to dilute the evidence. After Whitecourt, the river ran through the wilderness for another 196 kilometres (122 miles) before it even crossed under the first significant highway bridge and then onto another community down-stream. Altogether it would be a total of over 560 kilometres (348 miles) from Hinton before it ran through a town, that being Athabasca, Alberta.

It was a perfect scheme—and it would save the company a few million dollars in not having to dispose of the effluent safely and legally, and our politicians were all too eager to assist them in committing this crime. And it was a crime, ex-cept that they had a permit to commit the crime.

If a private citizen spilled even one barrel of caustic soda, roughly 200 litres (45 gallons), into that river, they would face jail time, and the pious government would spare no expense in making an example of them in the media. All the while, they were planning this *horrendous* act to destroy nature, because it was convenient and cheap and didn't cut into profits.

If you detect a slightly elevated annoyance in my script, it's because I am reliving those events as I type this, and quite frankly, this *hypocrisy* disgusts me. And this wasn't the first time this had happened, which is why I knew this was a real scenario.

When I was going to the Forestry School in Hinton, Alberta, in 1976, the instructors there briefed us on a similar incident. It took place two or three years earlier in the early 1970s, and it involved the previous owners of the pulp mill, St. Regis Pulp and Paper.

It turned out that one of the local, new Forest Officers happened to be down by the river very early one morning and noticed this black sludge drifting downstream. He quickly took water samples and followed it to the source to discover that the pulp mill had used a track hoe and trenched a significant gap in the wall of their settling ponds to drain it right into the river. A *horrendous* violation of the Environmental Act and Federal Fisheries Act, and they had them cold, or so the young ranger thought.

When it went to trial, the defense for the pulp mill claimed that because he never took a water sample upstream of the mill on that same day, there was no proof that it was coming from St. Regis Pulp and Paper. Despite the eye witness and the large trench dug into the side of the settling ponds, and the empty settling ponds. The judge then threw the case out of court. That shows you exactly who owns the government and the courts of Alberta. It's the industry, not the public!

So shortly after that court case, that young ranger was given 30 days to fill his new posting in Fort Chip, the north easternmost remote forest office in Alberta. He had a young family and didn't want to subject them to that isolation, which was, in actuality, a punishment for him doing his job to protect the environment, so he quit. They knew he would resign, which is why they did this. They wouldn't want to create a noisy public outcry for firing him for doing his job.

We were told this story to make us aware of exactly how the government works when big-industry is involved, and that we need to watch what we do because we can't expect the government, we worked for to back us up.

I asked Bob why he was telling me this, and he said it was because he couldn't do anything, and he thought someone else should know. Of course, that wasn't where he expected it to stop either as Bob was an intelligent guy. I left his office and went back to my own, thoroughly tormented by what was going to happen. I couldn't expose it to the media, as they would ask where I got the information, and that would mean the end of both our jobs, and I couldn't do that to him. He may not have been able to stop it or speak out, but he was brave enough to inform someone else whom he hoped would do something. Yeah, I know I was a sacrificial lamb, but it took courage on Bob's part in my books, for even trying this, and trusting me with the information.

His hands were tied as Bob would not only get fired, he would get prosecuted for violating the Secrecies Act that bound public servants not to divulge any internally disseminated information, and this qualified. You see, back in 1988, there was no such thing as whistleblower protection in Alberta. It never came into effect until 2012, a little behind the times for western democracy. But then seeing as to what's happening in North America these days, where people are headhunting for any whistleblower, to protect corruption, it's par for the course I guess for governments or industry that are doing things they know the public wouldn't approve of.

This situation tormented me for the next two days, and I had no idea what I could do about it. Praying about it was the only way to get any peace in my spirit and asking God, "How do I do this? How do I affect a change to this disastrous outcome, and not sacrifice myself and my family in the process?"

Knowing something is so wrong, and knowing how to stop it, are two concepts that are often very far apart, in our abilities to intervene. Being intelligent and being smart are actually two different things. In contrast, intelligence might give you the knowledge as to right and wrong; being smart would equip you to act on it without experiencing collateral damage for doing the right thing. I felt I was at a disadvantage in the smart's aspect for this one.

Then one day at work, I was listening to the radio as I might normally do while working on maps. The local radio station from Edson, Alberta, was having a call-in show, as they would every week, and announced that their next guest would be Dr. Ian Reid. They announced that he was the newly appointed Minister of Environment, who had moved from the Solicitor General portfolio, which he had held for many years. He was also the elected representative of the Yellowhead Region. Edson and Hinton were the two major towns, and the Weldwood Pulp Mill was one of the major industries.

There was going to be a provincial election coming in the spring of 1989, and Mr. Reid was out to do a little politicking and schmoozing with his constituency on the call-in show. He had been elected for three terms already and fully expected to win a fourth, virtually uncontested.

So, tell me, what do you think as a reader? Minister Reid was previously Solicitor General for the province in charge of upholding the law and ensuring those who violate it, were punished. He was now the Minister of Environment in charge of enforcing all environmental regulations and ensuring those who violated those regulations, were charged and punished. He was also the Member of Parliament for this region, and any industrial expansion would need government approval, and that would start with the local representative.

Do you think he knew that his department had issued this permit, which would have had to be signed off by the Minister in Charge? Meaning it was him, of course, as the Minister of the Environment! Do you think he knew this was violating the Environmental Act? And as former Solicitor General, do you think he knew it was a violation that would warrant prosecution? If you answered "no," maybe, re-read this story again.

As soon as I heard this on the radio, my inner voice was screaming at me, saying, *"This is it—this is how you can expose this and maybe do it anonymously."*

My heart was racing at that point, and I left the outer office and went into my own private office and closed the door, and turned on my radio to the local station. I can't express how terrified I was at this point, not only my career, but my freedom would be at stake, as I would be prosecuted and made an example of, and so would Bob.

As the call-in show started, the customary greetings took place with Mr. Reid, and the local callers were congratulating him on such a marvelous job he was doing for our region, then I finally got through. There was a cue, but back then, there was no seven-second delay, as there is on call-in shows today, where they can cut you off before your comment gets aired. I knew I was doing the right thing morally, ethically, and even legally as far as the Environmental Act was concerned. But I was terrified of doing it because I knew the government would never want the public to see the truth and would make an example of anyone who exposed their wrongdoing. But you know what bothered me about it the most at that moment? You'll laugh—I was concerned because I would have to lie and give them a false name.

That wouldn't have been a problem for most of my fellow government employees at the time, but it bothered me back then. That may seem ironic, but being smart right then was more important than taking the high moral route and exposing who I was, as my goal was not to be a martyr.

I understood that there would be a very high price to be paid if I chose to do the right thing, and anyone found out. That's what it's like when you work for corrupt organizations, and they exist in every walk of life, and especially in government.

I can't say I would be as tormented about the risk today, under the same circumstances, as I've seen a lot of corruption in the decades since then. I also had to try and change my voice a bit, and since I had been guiding several Americans for moose hunting (that's in my other book), I put on my best East Texas accent, when I started talking.

I started by congratulating Mr. Reid on his appointment to Environment Minister, to which he gave his obligatory appreciation. Then I asked if he knew about the expansion project for Weldwood Lumber, who now owned the pulp mill. He said he did and then bragged that he'd worked closely with them during the transition and now with plans for the expansion, which would increase job opportunities in the area.

I then asked him if he knew what they were going to do with their caustic soda settling ponds as they needed to expand them as well. There was a little pause—and then he said that he didn't know the *details*, but he was sure it would meet all government regulations.

I said, "You should know the details as you are not only the Member of Parliament for this region but also the Environment Minister in charge of protecting the environment on behalf of the people of Alberta."

He replied that he was familiar with their request to expand the ponds and that he didn't know exactly how they would do it.

I said, "I knew exactly how it would be done because I work in this industry." I added that they had a written permit from the Department of Environment, signed by him to take a couple of track hoes and trench the settling ponds directly into the Athabasca River at 3 a.m. on Sunday. That's when they hoped no one would be around to notice it, and no one would be privy to the documents, as protected under the government's Privacy Act.

I then berated him for allowing such an egregious breach of environmental policy and signing off on this *despicable* act. The radio host suddenly cut in and said that they had to break for a commercial, and would be back with Minister Reid after the break.

I had so much adrenalin pumping through me at that point that my whole body was shaking. *I had done it.* I had exposed this act and the hypocrisy of the department and, in some small way, vindicated that young forest officer who lost his job more than a decade earlier. I hoped, in some way, he'd find out what had happened this time they tried it and would feel good about it.

When the commercial break was over, the radio host said that Mr. Reid had been called away to other duties, and could no longer continue with the call-in show. I suspect that their phone lines were all lit up after my call, and he didn't want to answer any more questions from anyone regarding what he knew was happening. I also understand that he had some reasonably contentious people at his constituency meetings on the run-up to the election.

So, I had done my part and couldn't do, anymore, but this wasn't over obviously. That Sunday in question, before 3 a.m., a group of people from the town of Hinton were at the river with cameras. Weldwood didn't dare open up those settling ponds, even though they had a permit from the Ministry of Environment to do so, showing just how *wrong* they knew their activity was going to be. And this had been stopped!

The following information is from an old website called *Friends of the Athabasca* or FOTA, which existed from the fall of 1988 to 2009:

> Friends of the Athabasca Environmental Association (FOTA) was formed in the fall of 1988 in Alberta as a reaction to the activities of the bleach kraft pulp and paper industry on the Athabasca River Basin. Their efforts were later instrumental in forcing new environmental guidelines to be enacted to protect the river prior to the announcement of the construction of a new bleach kraft mill near the town of Athabasca in January of 1990. Concerned Citizens of the Athabasca River basin felt that there was little public input in the process of locating another mill on the Athabasca River and joined together to form a non-profit chartered society. Founded by Louis Schmittroth, the association was active in criticizing massive pulp, paper, and industrial forestry expansion in the boreal forest, and called for a more measured approach to development that would protect the ecosystem in the Athabasca area.

This environmentally responsible action by FOTA is what my actions spawned, and there have been many offshoot groups like it around the world. It has helped ensure that rivers in that part of Alberta received better protections, and "Friends of Rivers" groups all over the world have sprung up since then doing the same, protecting the environment from corrupt industrial practices. It was because of my actions, and yet I could tell no one.

I was scared in the days following as the government was passing around a sound recording of the show, to the various offices in the region, trying to identify who the caller was, as they suspected it must be a government employee since the person knew the details of the permit. It was a concerted headhunt for whoever exposed their corruption, and they wanted a *sacrificial lamb* as an example to the rest. No one asked me directly, though; after all, I was just a mapping technician by then having switched from a forest officer's position a year earlier. I was not privy to any environmental policies or permits being issued at that point, so I did not need to lie to anyone.

A week later, I saw Bob again by chance, and he smiled at me. Then he said that he heard that a bunch of people went down to the effluent ponds and stopped them from dumping into the

Athabasca. He had heard that an anonymous caller tipped them off on a call-in show on the Edson radio station. I looked at him, and without breaking a smile, I just said, "imagine that." Bob smiled at me and winked, and then we parted ways.

You could, of course, judge me by saying I willingly broke the confidentiality of the government permit, and therefore I was in the wrong, and shame on me, I should repent.

In that case, we must part ways based on our personal definition of what having *integrity* actually means. To me, "it means doing the right thing, regardless of the rules put in place to protect the corrupt and the potential cost to one's self." The excuse of "I was just following orders" has been used to justify atrocities of all kinds throughout history. And to me, those people never had integrity, and I don't believe God would see it that way either.

For Christians, we know that Jesus could have escaped being crucified if he simply denied the claims against him and went along with the demands of the authorities of the day. He had integrity and did what was right, despite the personal cost.

I believe I escaped retribution, only because I had Divine protection at the time, and was smart enough not to gloat about my victory to anyone, not even my family. As I said, being intelligent, and being smart are two different things, as no one ever accused me of being too intelligent.

So, my readers, I'd like to say that God will only use you to the capacity that he knows you are capable of taking action. The ability—God knows you are capable of, not the limits of what you think you can achieve. It can be exhilarating or downright terrifying, but it will always be worth it to your soul if not to your physical well-being, financially, or your emotional state. You might never make a penny off of your efforts, like me, but the knowledge that you did the right thing is invaluable and a treasure you will always have with you, even if no one else will ever know. And, your actions may just help someone else to make the right decisions in life as well.

I have only told this story to perhaps three people in my life and asked them all to keep it confidential as I was still trying to make a living in environmental work. I have discovered that even working as a consultant, most companies don't want you to do the right thing, as a professional upholding the regulations. They want you to be loyal to your paycheque and use creativity to hide what you find that is wrong. They view your job as being able to keep them out of trouble by any means and save them money, even by violating regulations—even government environmental auditing authorities think the same way.

It's been a struggle both financially and emotionally at times these last two or three decades, but I have my memories of how God was close to me in the past and provided for me in many ways so that I could provide for my family. Am I living the life of a saint? Far from it! I have the same struggles as everyone else, but I can go back to the times when I did trust in *divine intervention* to help me make it through and hang onto those memories until I depart this world.

I hope that you know of someone else who could use the encouragement that these stories might provide, in that there is always someone watching out for you in every kind of situation in life, and when you need help, all you need to do is ask, and trust, and it will be there.

By the way, Minister Reid lost the election that next spring after three terms in office. His party stayed in power, but it seems the local constituents weren't particularly enamoured with his behaviour anymore! Such are the choices in life we make when we think we can't be touched, and it leads to an outcome we never anticipated!

# CHAPTER TWELVE

# Cut the Rope

This story involves several decisions I had made that turned out differently than I had anticipated. And in a roundabout way, the spirit was trying to convince me of my mistake and to trust God. You'll see how stubborn I can be, or maybe you'll just be looking in a mirror as you read it. If so, realize there is always a way out, and something else is waiting for you that is better. You might find it interesting as this was another major turning point in my life.

I had been with the Forest Service in Whitecourt, Alberta, for nearly a decade, and although a change over to a mapping technician was more palatable, I wasn't thrilled. Yes, I was very good with aerial photography and mapping and enjoyed the work, and I also didn't have to go on the fire line anymore. Yes, some might say I was a pansy, but it wasn't the working conditions I hated, as I grew up in harsher conditions than that. It was that I was away from my wife and my little ones all summer on fire action, or waiting on standby at some remote location. Seeing them for only a couple days every three weeks in some summers or always being on call on weekends meant we never had a single summer vacation in eight years, and that wasn't my idea of raising children.

I wanted to quit the Forest Service and had many urgings by my inner voice to do so, but was afraid to take action. I didn't know where else I could go as the economy was in a downturn. Imagine that, after all the times that I believed *divine intervention* was guiding me, I still had doubts. That's because I'm human, I guess, and still struggling with confidence. So, don't feel bad if you haven't achieved perfection yet, we're not all built the same. Anyone who says they never have any doubts or worries, is either far more confident than the majority of people could ever be, or they're just trying to impress you for some other reason, and they aren't being truthful. I don't believe there is a third choice, so you pick!

There was a new thermal, mechanical pulp mill soon to be starting production in Whitecourt at the time, and they were hiring people to go through training to be a millwright. Starting salary was double what I made as a public servant. I knew one other Forest Officer who had jumped ship, at my urging and was selected to receive the training. I had encouraged him to throw his name into the hat after he came to me and said he didn't know what to do and was worried. He and his wife both worked, and they had a beautiful place south of Whitecourt, where they raised Arabian horses and gave riding lessons.

Cliff H. had traded him off for another Forest Officer who played hockey. Yes, you read that right. The Forest Service had a volunteer men's hockey team, and Cliff H. fancied himself a general manager. The forest superintendents traded forest officers like they were hockey players, except of course they never got the salary of hockey players to compensate for being uprooted on short notice and having to sell their property and start over. He and his wife didn't want to give up what they had built up to move to a very small community in the Rocky Mountain House Forest District, which they had 30 days to move, so he jumped ship.

Being traded, for a different reason, was how I ended up switching from being a Forest Officer to a lesser position as a mapping technician. Provincial Headquarters had requested that the Whitecourt Forest create the first designated

Recreational Snowmobile Trail System in the province, and I was given the task because of my ability to work with aerial photography and locate the best routes to make a series of looped trails. Plus, I had just completed the Sand Hills Cross Country Ski Trail System east of Whitecourt, which became so popular that is was written up in outdoor magazines back then, and they even had provincial competitions there.

The Athabasca Snowmobile Trail System got featured in snowmobile magazines and was where provincial competitions were held as well. So, what did all that exceptional work get me you might wonder, it got me *traded*. That's right; another forest wanted a similar trail system, so they convinced the forest superintendent in Whitecourt, to trade me. This scenario was a problem for me because two months earlier, we had just bought a quarter section of land and moved our house trailer onto it. If we tried to sell it now, we'd "lose our shirt," as the saying goes.

When I told the superintendent and my chief ranger about the land and how we'd lose out financially, they were livid. I didn't know it at the time, but the only reason they could not force you to move back then was a financial hardship. The superintendent said to me, "You never told me you were going to buy a piece of property."

To which I replied, "I didn't know I was required to tell the government that I was buying anything, let alone a piece of property to live on?" And of course, I was right. So, they said they'd give me one year to sell the property and then they would move me.

I can tell you that it created a lot of stress for me at the time, and I didn't know what to do. Then, only a few days later, the thought came to me (that inner voice again) that I should go and ask the current mapping technician if he wanted to switch jobs, as he'd always wanted to be a Forest Officer. So, I went to him and said that perhaps in six or eight months we could switch jobs. I knew management would go for it because I was far more skilled at working with aerial photography and maps than he was. They could then have me design the trail systems for other districts from my position as a mapping technician out of the Regional Headquarters in Whitecourt.

It was only four days later that they came to me and said I was switching positions, as the mapping technician couldn't wait. For me, it was *divine intervention* that gave me the idea to ask to trade jobs as I had never heard of that option before. And when God does something, it usually happens fast, as you've read in previous stories in this book.

However, in my new position, I also didn't get any overtime, and the loss of that extra income was hard on a family where there is only one person with a salary, so money was also a motivator for me. Millar Western had already chosen their 45 people to go through the training, 15 per shift. I was a little late to the game, even though the training didn't start until the end of March.

I thought, why not try anyway and I sent in an application. After much prayer and pleading with God, demanding this new job with far better pay, I received a call for an interview, and they had bumped someone else and gave me the position. So, I got what I wanted!

I was quite excited and looking forward to it, although I had no mechanical background. But maybe because my dad was a millwright in a pulp mill in The Pas, Manitoba, I had some hereditary advantage in understanding the technology, or so I half-heartedly hoped. But a pre-existing knowledge of machinery and mechanics wasn't needed as the preparation was thorough. They had everyone from truckers to painters to unemployed factory workers and even a pizza delivery guy hired for the training, and I was curious about the quality of their hiring criteria. No wonder they bumped someone for a person with a college diploma, and experience as a forest officer and mapping technician, and had run his own small mapping company for a couple of years.

Then a series of small events started to change the atmosphere for me. After a month of group training, the company wanted the new millwrights to select a spokesperson for the group to bring grievances to the management, as well as positive suggestions in the work environment. It was a silent vote, with no one putting their name up for the position.

To my dismay, they selected me. So, either the group thought my years as a Forest Officer looking after fire crews, summer work crews, and supervising companies in the oil field and logging operations would be a benefit to them. Or I was the sacrificial lamb to the slaughter, and I came to think of the position that way. It came with no perks, and since my supervisor was younger than me, he felt he had something to prove, so he gave me the crappiest job in the mill. While everyone else was working on the automated equipment which the training had been for, I was sweeping floors and shovelling hot wet pulp, every hour of every day for every shift, without end, for my entire time there.

On top of that, my feet started to always hurt while on shift. I thought it must have been the concrete floors as I was used to walking many miles every day in the bush all year, with no indication of tendonitis in my feet, but I had it big time. I also had great difficulty staying awake on the 25-minute drive home after a night shift. At least once every week, sometimes two or three times, I would wake up as my car tire slipped off the pavement on the way home, in the opposite lane across the highway. A head-on collision was in my future for sure, and it was the ridiculous work schedule that caused it, I told myself.

We worked 12-hour shifts and had three days on nights, one day off, then three days on day shift, two days off, then three days on nights again, round and round it went. Having only one day to switch a sleep pattern was difficult for me, and falling asleep when driving was now almost a daily occurrence—that doesn't bode well for long-term employment, or a long life, at least not for me.

I also had a problem with the feeling that everyone else thought I was just there to clean up for them. On one occasion, I was called by the control room to head up to the wet end of the mill, as there was a problem for which they needed help. So, I dutifully trudged over there and up three levels of stairs to find one of the wet end shift guys standing beside a pile of wet pulp about the size that would fill three wheelbarrows. He was holding a scoop shovel, and when I approached, he handed me the shovel and told me to shovel it back into the hopper—just four feet away. I was stunned at his utter laziness as he stood there and watched as I shovelled the pulp, and I thought, why am I the rep for these guys that couldn't qualify for any job I'd done in the past?

One night around 3 a.m., I was walking between large electric motors that were screaming away on the ground floor and talking to God in my head. Where I was working, we needed constant ear protection all shift, which was a bit of a change from being in the silence of the forest most of the time and enjoying the peacefulness, and quiet. As I walked past the electric motors in the 40 degrees Celsius (104°F) temperatures and sweltering humidity from the hot wet pulp, I said to myself, "What am I doing here?"

As clear as day, the response came back, *"You wanted the big bucks."*

I stopped in my tracks, kind of stunned by that answer, and said, "I don't belong here."

And the response was, *"That's right. You don't."* My heart sank as I realized the truth.

Yes, the money was good, but I had spent two months doing nothing but sweeping and shovelling as a trained millwright no less. It didn't seem like it was going to change because my supervisor was not happy that the millwright representative was on his shift, and I was older than he was by four years. Money is one thing, and it's something I never had much of, but job satisfaction is more important, I think. If you spend your whole career in a job you hate, what's the point of subjecting yourself to that and being unhappy throughout your life? But with no place to go, what do you do, I thought, but stick with it.

I stressed over this for the next couple of days and told Pastor George Stone about it, at the little independent church near Peers, Alberta, close to where we were living out in the country. I said to him that I didn't believe I was supposed to be working where I was, but I feel like I'm hanging onto the end of a rope and can't let go.

I was waiting for his helpful and encouraging advice, which would calm my anxiety and show me what I should do. His response was, *"I guess I'll have to pray that God cuts the rope then!"* As my eyes widened, I realized that wasn't the consoling wisdom I was hoping for, and I was a little shocked! But Pastor Stone knew what he was saying!

So, I went back to work and a day later made the decision that I would stick with this until the middle of September and then quit, I promised myself, and whoever else was listening to my thoughts. I looked at the work schedule and saw the day would be September 12. It gave me some comfort that I had made a decision, and the date set to leave that place.

Over the next two months, everything seemed to go a little better. My feet weren't hurting as much, I got to spend some time operating the forklifts loading the train cars in the dry end of the plant, and I hadn't fallen asleep, hardly at all, on the drive home. I had forgotten all about quitting, and as I started one-night shift, I was reminded by that inner voice that it was September 12. Oh yeah, I thought I was going to quit today.

But everything seemed to be going okay. So, maybe I'll stick it out until Christmas, the extra money would help. Yeah, I know what you're thinking. I had made a *promise*, not just to myself, but to God, and now I was backing out of it—right, but it was only three more months, what could it hurt?

That night one of the big grinders got impacted with pulp when not enough water was flowing through it, and a mechanic asked me to help him clear it. He disassembled the top section, and we started to cut out the dry pulp. It took us until about 11 p.m., and he had been on overtime since his shift ended at 7 p.m.

He then turned to me and said, "You can give me a ride home in one of the company trucks."

I said, "Are you sure that's allowed?"

To which he replied, "I always get one of the guys to drive me home if I've worked late." Okay, I thought, I'll give you a ride. It was just to the top of the hill in town, literally only 2.7 kilometres (1.68 miles), and I was back at the mill in about five minutes round trip. But as I walked into the large open door at the dry end, my supervisor, John, was waiting for me.

He was steaming mad, but I suspected quite happy inside as he took a strip off of me for leaving the plant. I told him what had happened and what the millwright had said, but he didn't care. He said this was going on my permanent record, and I would be officially reprimanded. I guess pushing a broom was critical to the plant's operation. He then said that he had a job for me first and walked over to the repulper and told me to get a ladder and get up on top of there and shovel that off. As it turned out, the minute I left the plant, this repulper burped and spewed out about 2,720 kilograms (6,000 pounds) of hot wet pulp. And he immediately started looking for his shovel monkey! Coincidence, I don't think so?

There was a mountain of wet pulp up there covering an area about 3.7 metres square (12x12 feet), and it was piled 1.4 metres (5 feet) deep. Located right over a digester and the temperatures were around 49 degrees Celsius (120°F) and had hot steam rising steadily. Now I have sympathy for steamed vegetables and will never scorn a lobster as it dies. So, I climbed up and started shovelling, and was once again reminded that I was supposed to quit today. I struggled with the conversation for an hour or two as I shovelled pulp and then realized the truth. I stopped shovelling and said to God, "If I don't quit, you're going to cut the rope, aren't you?"

The response was, *"Yes."* Okay, I thought to myself, if I'm not supposed to be here, I'll quit after this shift. Instantly I had a vision of me letting go of a rope and falling. It was so clear and vivid in my mind that I staggered backward to catch my balance and nearly fell off the repulper; since this time, God knew I meant it!

I was startled by the experience but also a bit relieved. I started singing a gospel song to myself at the time as I worked on finishing my job, and soaked to the skin from the steam and heat. When I came down from there, my supervisor found me again and motioned for me to follow him to the other end of the plant on the ground floor. It was near an open door on the west side of the mill, and he told me to keep debris from clogging the floor drains as the water from a spill worked its way down here. He then added that he'd be putting my reprimand on my file in the morning, and I'd have to see the General Manager.

So, I stood guard over floor drains for the rest of the shift and talked to God. I wanted some confirmation that I was making the right decision, remembering the *fleece* I'd used in the past, so I asked for it. I knew my supervisor would not typically ever come down to this end of the plant, as he supervised the dry end. The only reason I was here was the control room asked if he could get someone to help with the drains, and so he did. I put up a *fleece* in that; "if he came by here again, I would tell him I was quitting today." By saying it to someone, that act wouldn't allow me to change my mind after the shift. And so, I waited and dutifully pulled a little debris out of the drain every hour.

I didn't know what I would do for a job after I quit. I couldn't go back to the Forest Service, they had filled my position already, but I knew I wasn't supposed to be here. I wanted to be wherever God wanted me to be, and as scary as that was, I knew it was the right decision. As the time ticked by and he hadn't shown up, I was wondering about my decision, and then with less than ten minutes left in the shift, my supervisor came walking down the hallway towards me, and I knew God had sent him. He was probably hoping to catch me missing from my essential post on drain watch, so he had something more he could add to my reprimand. I told him I needed to speak to him outside, so I turned and walked to the open door, just 6 metres (20 feet) away. And he followed. It was too noisy inside for a conversation, but I wondered what he was expecting me to do.

I told him that he'd have to find someone else to replace me for the next shift if anyone even needs to, as I won't be coming back after today. This response caught him totally off guard, and he started saying that I didn't have to worry, he wouldn't be putting anything on my record; they don't even need to know what happened and that it wasn't a severe issue anyway. I could tell he was very nervous at hearing my decision and was trying his best to reverse it, but what's that old saying, "Too little too late!"

I said I appreciated that, but I've had enough. This job isn't what I expected it to be, and I didn't plan on spending the rest of my career at the end of a broom. My supervisor obviously didn't want to explain to management why the guy they picked at the last minute and who the millwrights picked to be their representative was now quitting. I also suspect he didn't want to tell management what his part was in causing it.

To try and ease his mind, I said that this has nothing to do with him, it's a decision I had to make a long time ago; he just made it easier for me to follow through. He asked me to take tomorrow off as a sick day and think about it, and we'd talk next week. I said I wouldn't be here next week, but thanks for the offer, and you can tell management that I quit. With that, I thanked him for listening, and I left to go to the locker room to leave my work coveralls and hard hat behind, and take my padlock off the locker.

In the locker room, I only told the young guy from the Forest Service, who was a friend, and was coming in on the next shift. He was stunned and asked what I would do now? I said I didn't know, but I know I'm not supposed to be here. I had a couple of telephone calls from the management by the time I got home. They were asking me to come in so they could discuss the problems and promised me that within a couple of weeks, they would move me up to the control room. It would be higher pay and more responsibility than clean up as it was a supervisory position. I said thanks, but no, I won't be returning.

I found out years later, actually about 12 years later, when we returned to the Whitecourt area as my son Justin was buying some purebred South African Boar goats from a guy south of town, that I was famous. When the guy we were buying the goats from heard my name, he asked if I had ever worked at the pulp mill in Whitecourt. And I said I had, at the very beginning, when it opened. He smiled and said, *"You're Famous."*

I chuckled and asked why. He said that he worked there, and everyone wanted to know who the first guy to quit was, and why! And they also wanted to know how it worked out. I told him of the adventures I had been on and my own business that had paid me many times what Millar Western would have, and he said he'd pass it on to the rest. I guess people working there needed a reason to hope, and to break free as well, sometimes.

So, as you read this, my friend, I can tell you that you've listened to a large part of my life that usually isn't told to strangers. What do you think? Why did I have that conversation that night walking between the electric motors and especially all the trouble with my feet and then dangerously falling asleep on the way home after almost every morning shift?

By the way, it has been 32 years since then, and I have never fallen asleep at the wheel since, and I have made some 24-hour drives without stopping for a rest. But I couldn't make it 32 kilometres (20 miles) without falling asleep after working a 12-hour shift at Millar Western.

The guidance from Pastor Stone was an ultimatum from God that if I didn't quit, he was going to *cut the rope*. Then the day of reckoning came, and when all was going well, and I decided to stay, everything suddenly went to hell in short order. And when I realized what was happening and agreed to follow through on my promise, I had a waking vision of letting go of a rope that was so real at the moment that I began to fall physically. Then God had met the *fleece* I put up to confirm my decision when I saw the supervisor before the end of the shift?

Sometimes one has to concede that there are circumstances in life where *divine intervention* was the only answer. Please remember it is available for everyone willing to ask for it, no matter what you claim to believe.

# CHAPTER THIRTEEN

# Meeting a Milestone

After leaving Millar Western's new thermal, mechanical pulp mill, I didn't have a clue what I would do for a living. The next week I was trying to think of people I might call in the resource inventory field. And could only think of one person who worked for the Canadian Federal Forest Service, whom I had talked to a decade before when I had found out about a Yukon contract, which I was successful at winning. So, I looked up a number for him and made the call.

He told me that he had nothing federally available but, he'd heard that Alberta was starting up a mapping inventory of what they called the White Zone in the province, requiring aerial photo interpreters. I got in touch with the people who were putting it together and found out that the allocation under contract would go to the winning bid of just one company. The task then was to gather together enough interpreters from the old Alberta Phase III program and put together a team to bid on the work.

A few of us got together, and I tried to convince them that we could form our own company and bid on the contract ourselves, but they were reluctant to do so. All they wanted to do was subcontract to another company that was bidding on the project. Okay, I thought, if that's the best we can do, then let's give them a price per township, which was 93 square kilometres (36 square miles) of area. We each said how much work we thought we could finish per month, to put that into the contract bid. I had said I could easily do 390 square kilometres (about 150 sq. miles) per month, to which some snickered, and others said, "We've got to be realistic here, and we also have to divide up the work evenly." Alright, I'll go along with that, and they all decided they could manage two map sheets or just 186 square kilometres (72 sq. miles) per month. The company could then put that in their bid and also bid for producing all the mapping and digital files as well.

There was a second company that was also favoured to win. It was from Ontario and had connections with the supervisor of the project, Richard, the same guy who tried to blackmail me many years before. But both companies needed us as experienced photo interpreters from Alberta to bid with them, so we gave them both the same price.

One of the two companies won, of course, as they were the only ones that included the Phase III inventory photo interpreters. But after they won, the company called us in for a meeting. It turns out that their professional forester had made a severe math error when they made their bid. They felt they wouldn't make as much profit as they planned, so they asked the interpreters to cut their price per map sheet.

This change didn't go over well, but we managed to come to a compromise and settled on a price that would work for us. All the photo interpreters in our group agreed to do the work for a ten percent reduction per map sheet, and it was unanimous. So, we were given the aerial photography for four map sheets each to start or work in separate areas of the province, to delineate the forest into different stands down to 2 hectares (5 acres) in size. And then, we had to establish ten ground plots per township to gather field data on tree ages, heights, species composition, as reference data. And then start classifying the forest cover and applying forest descriptions as to density, height, age, composition, etc.

I was keen to get going since it was already November, and I had been out of work for two months, so I started right away and was soon sending in townships for evaluation. After an internal audit to check the accuracy, they would go to the mapping stage. About six weeks later, I asked the manager how the project was progressing, and he told me that I was the only interpreter out of seven who had handed in any work. As time went on and I checked again in another two weeks, the answer was still the same.

The manager was concerned as they had production milestones they had to meet on the contract. I contacted all of the interpreters to ask why they weren't handing in any work, and they had a variety of reasons. They were taking a holiday before starting, or they had other work to finish up first, or they had classes to attend so they couldn't get at it, or a myriad of other excuses. I thought, why did everyone say they could work on the contract if they knew they didn't have the time for it? They knew that there were production deadlines in place even before we placed the bid.

But one of them confided in me that they had made a backdoor deal with Richard from the government, who had wanted the other company to win the contract. And if the company who had won the project didn't meet their first production milestone of 15 townships in three months, they would forfeit the contract to the next bidder. They were considerably more expensive, but as photo interpreters, we would get our ten percent back.

Okay, I'm not opposed to making more money, especially since the error was not ours. However, we had all agreed together to undertake the project for the ten percent reduction. If you give your word to do work for an agreed-upon price, regardless of the circumstances, that should mean something, at least if a person had any integrity. They were intentionally sabotaging the contract at Richard's urging, and I suspected an under the table deal was going on between Richard and the company from Ontario. I also realized that because Richard knew my character, he had instructed the rest not to talk to me and that he wouldn't include me in the scheme.

Most of the photo interpreters in our group knew me as someone who would not compromise integrity for personal benefit or to suck up to someone else. There was one person that had worked on the Phase III project after I had quit, who didn't know me. He was the one who "spilled the beans" to me, thinking I would go along with all the rest—big mistake because that's not who I am!

I was also of the understanding that if Richard got his way and forced the contract to be turned over to the other company, his favourite bidder; they might feel they didn't need seven interpreters. And could do without me, even though he knew that I could do more than twice the production of anyone else. I had a family to support and believed that God had given me this opportunity, and this was precisely why I was required to leave Millar Western when I did because God knew this contract was coming up, and he knew that I loved this work and was very good at it.

I went to the manager of the company and informed him that the rest of the interpreters had been convinced by Richard to throw the contract by ensuring they never met the first production milestone in time. He was perplexed as to how do you convince six other people, whom you couldn't replace because they were required in terms of the contract, to please do what they had agreed to do? In short, you can't!

So, I told the manager to give me all the map sheets I could handle, and I would meet their deadline on my own. I received another 13 map sheets, and I had two months to do them and save the contract. I worked 16 to 18 hours a day and completed 1,400 square kilometres (roughly 540 sq. miles) in three months.

The government had to do the auditing, and Richard, continuously said there were too many errors, only to be challenged by me. They conducted actual field evaluations to settle the dispute, which proved I was right, and he was wrong. I knew he was trying to hold up the contract. Since my company manager knew what he was up to, he challenged every audit Richard conducted until he stopped trying to discredit my work, because of continually being proven wrong. It was becoming evident to everyone that something underhanded was at play.

I was interpreting 466 square kilometres (roughly 180 sq. miles) a month, and all audits passed after challenging the assessment by the government's expert, Richard. Since I had saved the contract, the company allowed me to take as many map sheets as I wanted in any area I wanted, and the rest of the interpreters who had conspired to sink the project could pick up what was left.

There were some sections of the White Zone in the province that had large areas of farmland and were much faster to interpret, but we still got the same amount of money per map sheet, and I picked as many of those as I could get. In 18 months, I completed 154 map sheets out of a total of 430.

And, after meeting the first deadline, I contacted a friend of mine named Jim P., who I had trained as a photo interpreter a decade before. He was then doing environmental work for a coal mine in southern B.C. I explained the situation and asked him to help me finish the contract as there were more production milestones to meet. Jim was already looking for a change, and my telephone call came at the right time. He was a high-quality aerial photo interpreter; I know because I trained him!

In those 18 months, Jim completed 106 map sheets. Between the two of us, we did 260 map sheets out of 430 or just over 60 percent of the workload out of a total of now eight aerial photo interpreters. We finished our areas two months before the rest of the interpreters finished theirs. I took only 1.5 days off in 18 months, averaging 14 hours a day bent over an Abrams stereoscope classifying forest cover.

Of course, the rest of the photo interpreters hated me, and they still do—to this day. But that's the nature of people who are lacking in morals and integrity. Their scheme did not work out well for them, and I was to blame in their eyes, even though they saw no problem in breaking their word and doing a deal under the table to sink a project.

Instead of the original 61 map sheets each, which we agreed to complete in dividing up the work evenly, I had taken the lion's share, but it was the only way to save the contract and provide for my family. We were getting $1,150 per map sheet, and after fieldwork costs, we would make a profit of about $950 per map sheet. In those 18 months, I made enough to build a brand-new house for my family, and pay off our land, and we sold our house trailer to a young couple for just $10,000.

Because I was willing to listen to that inner voice directing me to leave Millar Western when it seemed that I wasn't supposed to be there, I had made double the income in those 18 months that I would have at Millar Western and four times what I was making at the Forest Service. But I had to quit first, and trust that God would take care of my family and me.

It's not an easy thing to do folks, and I have struggled with that many times since, as I witnessed everything falling apart around me, on different occasions. But I can tell you that, despite the hardships and struggles and the feelings of despair, thinking that God or Universal Energy or my Guardian Angel or Spirit Guide (whatever terminology you want to use) might have forgotten about me. God never did.

These are cherished memories that I can hold onto, which testify to the faithfulness of the entity I call God, who provides *divine intervention* exactly when needed. Not before, and not too late, and not more than is necessary. But it often requires your efforts as well since nothing is free, and we only grow to appreciate what we have accomplished, by putting in the work needed.

You can agree or disagree or laugh or be skeptical. That's okay with me because I do not need you to agree with me for me to believe. These experiences in my life, the big ones and the little ones have convinced me that *divine intervention* is real beyond all doubt. If you choose not to believe it, then it only affects you, no one else!

# CHAPTER FOURTEEN

# Commentary on Unconditional Trust

After this happened and witnessing many instances of *divine intervention* showing the faithfulness of God in taking care of me in so many meaningful ways, I might claim that I have never doubted God again. I have always totally and completely trusted that I would be taken care of, and have never worried since, and neither should you.

If I were to make such a *claim*, it would be a bold-faced lie, and in my honest opinion, unrealistic for anyone to make that claim. Sure, right after everything has worked out wonderfully, and you're on a spiritual high, one might feel that way, and make that statement to everyone around them. After all, that's what giving a positive testimony—is all about, right?

That's why when miraculous events work out as prayed for; believers are encouraged to tell others as quickly as possible so that it can benefit their faith. It allows the listeners to feed off of the spiritual high and soak in some of that good energy, giving them confidence in their relationship with God! But it's not long-lasting for many people if it hasn't been their own experience. And sometimes, even if it has, the worries of life creep in quickly.

Saying that you never worry and neither should anyone else, might sound good on the surface, but to those who still do, and hear you say that, it makes them feel inadequate and wondering why they can't shake off the fears of life like you have, and they often feel like a failure.

Unfortunately, there are those self-righteous believers who would then accuse you of having too little faith if you continued to worry about things, which makes you feel even worse. If I had a scar for every religiously pious individual who has ever said to me that I had too little faith, I'd—oh, wait—I do have the scars! And yet, I have had more *miraculous* events take place in my life by trusting God and living by faith than most people I know of, who would then try and instruct me on how I should learn to trust God. We don't all walk in the same shoes or grow in our faith at the same rate, and we need to remember that when attempting to chastise or encourage one another.

I'm not willing to tell people that they have a lack of faith if they still worry and have doubts in their lives, or that they need to learn to trust God more if they want to grow in their faith. I don't walk in their shoes and haven't gone through the things they have. So how can I judge them, as I do not see the world through their eyes? What I have learned, though, is that if you become puffed up with pride, the world is there to deflate you when you need it, and sometimes the cost is high and does long-term damage.

If you think I had always learned to trust unconditionally and never faltered, then I have given you the wrong impression. To claim one has unconditional trust, means, there is never any doubt at any time. One may appear like that on the surface and make that claim to others to maintain an image, which they choose to cultivate. Especially if they want you to admire and follow them, but God knows their heart, knows the truth, and knows their motives.

To prove my point, I merely need to continue my stories, and you will see that when I do have worries and doubt, God is patient and willing to gently steer me in the right direction, even if it means I have to walk miles in the pouring rain or blinding snowstorms for God to get my attention. God is patient with you too! You are not letting God down in any way, by not living up to the standards that others claim you should be. As long as you are moving forward and trying, that's all God asks.

So, if you're ready for another real-life story of *divine intervention*, here it goes!

# CHAPTER FIFTEEN

# Constant Problems

After completing the work on the Alberta White Zone Inventory, I was once again out of work, and instead of patiently waiting for God to reveal something to me, I felt I had to keep trying to find whatever I could on my own. On one occasion, I sought work with a logging contractor. He had a small local timber permit, and I had known him from my days as a Forest Officer. I knew several small logging operators who had their own sawmills; during inspections, I'd find out what they were paying their fallers. One timber faller was getting $1 per tree for falling, topping, and delimbing trees, which was pretty good money if you worked hard.

The trees in the boreal forests weren't massive, like in the coastal areas of Western Canada. Mature lodgepole pine would range from about

25–60 centimetres (10–24 inches) in diameter at the stump, and a mature stand would average around 38 centimetres (15 inches) in diameter, with a height of 21–24 metres (70–80 feet). That's quite small compared to the lower interior of B.C. or the Coast.

I approached one operator who had two Timber jack tree skidders that ran long lines and chokers, but only one faller, and I knew he needed another one. I offered to fell, de-limb, and top trees for him and his second skidder operator, and he asked me what I thought was fair in return. I mentioned that I know another operator who pays $1 a tree, and he said that he knew him too. But let's see how well you do first. Okay, I thought, that's fair.

So, I took my own Husqvarna 272 chainsaw and met him at the cutblock at 8 a.m. By 6 p.m., I felled, limbed, and topped 408 pine trees that day, as the skidder operator was keeping the tally. So, we chatted at the end of the day, and he was impressed that I could do 400 trees, and he had about a month's work for me. I said I would do it for $0.25 per tree, which I thought was quite a bargain for him. But he was only willing to pay me $0.10 a tree. That would be a whole $40.80 for the 10-hour day using my own chainsaw. That would have been well below minimum wage, and

I never even bothered to invoice him and never went back.

When someone so blatantly wants to take advantage of you, walk away. Do you remember my experience with Rhodes Vaugh Structural Steel as a draftsman—I did at that moment, and I still had a lot to learn it seemed?

I was contacted by Tim J., who was a long-time friend and now the Forester in Edson for a new lumber mill there, and he asked me if I would do regeneration surveys and cutblock lay-outs for them. I thought this opportunity was great and jumped at the chance. So, I showed up at their office, and he gave me the maps and said they would pay me daily as a contractor. Sounds good to me, I said, and I knew the standard rate for a contractor with his own truck, gas, and field equipment would be between $250 and $300 a day.

So, I went out and did a few days of cut-block layout for them, and at the end of the week I was to submit an invoice, so I discussed the payment with my good friend Tim. By the way, we were such "good friends" that when he moved to Edson, he phoned me and asked me to drive the 100 kilometres (60 miles) and unload his moving truck into his new house, since he had to go to work, and I did, all by myself—now that's a friend, wouldn't you say, as least from my side of the picture.

I asked him what he thought was fair, and he said they could pay me $130 a day in total. Yes, it was a lot more than $40.80 a day, but I was also using my truck and driving 170 kilometres (106 miles) one way to the cutblock area, and back home each day. It was making the days very long. After fuel costs, I was maybe making around $80 a day, and for 10- to 12-hour days, it was close to minimum wage, and that was for a person with two years of post-secondary forestry education and 12 years of working in forestry.

I was pretty disappointed at the time, but what else did I have for work, so I kept going. I had felt that I should not be there as I was being taken advantage of and by a long-term friend no less, who was probably making about $250 to $300 a day and given a company truck. After two to three months, I finally said I couldn't do this anymore, as I wasn't making any money. And besides that, I hadn't been paid in six weeks. Tim asked me what I needed, and I said at least $250 a day as that was the bottom of what the industry paid for contractors in my field. So, they agreed, and I continued, but my pay cheques were sporadic in coming.

I also began to notice that every single day something would go wrong. I would forget my equipment or my lunch I needed at home. Or I would forget my bush boots at home and have to work in my shoes all day, totally soaked. Or my truck would get stuck, and I needed to get pulled out, or I'd have a flat tire. I had flat tires three times in a row.

Then on different occasions, my battery would be dead when trying to get it started to get home at night. It got so bad that my friend Verne S. who also worked for that same company, would ask me, *"What went wrong today?"* whenever he'd answer a telephone call from me instead of saying hello.

I recalled that during the entire Alberta Green Zone Inventory, I had travelled the province from High Level, Alberta just below the NWT border to the USA border in the south and from the Saskatchewan border in the east to the B.C. border in the west. In summer rainstorms and winter blizzards, or when it was -40 degrees Celsius (-40°F) for weeks on end, and never once did I have a single problem with that same truck.

And yet, here I was having problems every single day. I slowly realized that God didn't want me there, but I was afraid to leave. I wasn't trusting God for anything better. Does this scenario sound familiar? On one of my last trips in early November, I had taken my wife's Isuzu Trooper 4x4 to do the final regen survey of the fall, or was it, scaling log decks, I can't remember exactly. When I got back to the vehicle at night, the battery was dead. And strangely enough, the second battery was also dead, as I had a spare 12-volt battery positioned under the hood connected to just the winch on a separate charging solenoid.

So, what now? It was raining hard by then, and of course, I had forgotten my rain gear, so I started to walk. I got to the main oilfield road and headed west in the dark. I had lots of time to think as I walked in the darkness, and the freezing rain soaked through me, thinking that perhaps God was trying to tell me something. I knew he was all along, but you can convince yourself that you don't hear it if you have enough fear that you don't know what else you can do. So, I decided I'd quit and trust that something would work out.

I managed to make it to an oilfield pumping station at about 10 p.m., and called Verne in Edson and told him where I was and my situation. Verne got to me around 11 p.m., and we drove back to where my vehicle was. He only had a two-wheel-drive company truck and short jumper cables, so he pulled up beside my truck, which was pointing into the trees when I parked. He boosted my vehicle, but then as he tried to move, he was stuck. Fortunately, since my truck was running now, I could pull him out with my 4x4, and we both went home.

To me, all those things going wrong every single day in the field was *divine intervention*. God was trying to let me know that I needed to trust him and walk away from this job, that I was only doing out of fear that God couldn't provide for me. If you witness a series of events going wrong for you where you work, and after you pray about it, it doesn't get better, be aware that maybe God is trying to get your attention, to step out of it in faith.

# CHAPTER SIXTEEN

# I Should Go Further

After deciding to quit working for the lumber company, since everything seemed to go wrong in the bush and I hadn't gotten paid in two months, it was getting obvious that God was trying to tell me something. Then Tim called one late November day and asked if I could please layout more cutblocks way down along the north bank of the Brazeau River. I was reluctant, but he said they would pay me $300 a day, but I had to use a snowmobile to get into the area as it was 8 kilometres (5 miles) from the end of vehicle access.

So, I agreed and then called Ted H., an old trapper and farmer friend of mine that lived about 16 kilometres (10 miles) away. He had a double-track Ski-doo, and I asked if I could rent it. He said, "no," but I could borrow it! Double track Ski-doo's are excellent in soft snow and just what

I needed, plus he was the only one I knew with a snowmobile.

The next day I was getting the rundown on the Ski-doo, and he told me he just changed the drive belt and put the old one in the toolbox on the machine. Even though I didn't own a snow-mobile, I was very familiar with them. My family had an old white Snow Cruiser when I was 14, and I drove it almost every day in the winter for years. Plus, the Forest Service had a couple of snowmobiles for us to use in winter to get into difficult areas.

I mentioned to Ted where I was going, and he said that he'd heard it was great elk country down by the Brazeau River, and mused that he always wanted to get a bull elk. I told him I was taking my rifle along, and if I tag anything, I will share it with him. So, we loaded the machine on-to a trailer I had, and I went home with it. I had convinced myself the trip was worth it as the late bull elk season was still on, and maybe I could bring back some meat.

The next morning it was a long drive of about 1.6 hours one way, and I got to the cut line that headed off the road to the south towards the Brazeau around 10:30 a.m. I unloaded the ma-chine, stowed my lunch, timber cruisers vest, spray paint cans, and hip chain gear in the storage compartment, and slung my rifle over my back before heading south towards the cutblocks I had to lay out.

I had gone around four miles south and then half a mile west when the machine started lugging and slowing down as I was climbing a hill. I kept going to get to the top, and at first, I suspected it was the deep soft snow that was the problem, especially going up the hills. But shortly after I reached the top, the machine stopped moving forward altogether. I could smell burning rubber, and that's never a good sign when you're on a snowmobile. I stopped and threw the hood open to see smoke billowing out, and after throwing snow on the belt and drive disc, I found that the brand-new drive belt had burned in half from the friction. Hmmm—this wasn't on the schedule for today, I thought!

After assessing the situation, I knew this wasn't good, but Ted told me he had put the old drive belt in the toolbox as a spare, so if I retrieved it and replaced the destroyed one, I would be all set. However, what are missing were the tools to take off the belt shield cover, as I found it to be bolted on very securely. I tried for a while to get them off but couldn't, and I was seriously stuck now as the snow started to fall lightly. As I stood there contemplating my next move, it was deathly quiet with no wind, and I then thought I could hear equipment working far to the north-west.

I knew the lumber company was logging in an area to the northwest, and this must be one of their big feller buncher units. So, I slung my .338 Mag over my shoulder and started walking to-wards the sound. It took me about an hour and forty-five minutes to get there as the depth of snow was over my knees. I was delayed for about ten minutes, when I came across a herd of wild horses that were curious about me, and I got a really good look at them from only 13 metres (15 yards) away. It was a surreal moment as we stared at each other for quite a while. I wished I had a camera to take pictures with the snow on the trees and a dozen wild horses pawing for food in the deep snow.

I continued towards the sound of the equipment and walked out of the timber right in front of the operator. He was quite stunned to see anyone come from that direction as there were no roads at all before the river about 11 kilometres (7 miles) away. I told him I was laying out their next cutblocks and what had happened, and then asked if I could borrow a variable wrench and a pair of pliers, which he gladly loaned to me. I said I would get them back to him through Tim or Verne, as I couldn't make it back here with the snowmobile since the trees are too dense. It was now around 1 p.m., and I then headed back to the stranded snowmobile. Arriving there, I changed out the belt, which took me about half an hour as I was unfamiliar with the old machine. Then I was in business again, and it was 3:15.

I knew I was experiencing problems because I wasn't putting my trust in God; and was putting up with this because I doubted, he would provide. Yes, even after everything I had been through in life, and witnessed some fantastic instances of *divine intervention* to work things out for me, I still doubted. Maybe you are perfect, but I'm not. I might not have been saying it out loud, but that is the apparent reason for my actions.

I thought right then that I should turn around and head back now and call it quits. I should have taken the hint from my *guardian angel*, as it was trying to spare me from what came next. With the problems I was having, I believe God was *shouting* at me by that time, but when you think you've got it all figured out and now under control, what do you do? I decided I should go further.

Another mile to the west and a mile south, I found the starting point of the cutblocks and placed some orange seismic ribbon on the corner of the cutblock, and painted the northwest corner and cutblock number on the tree with a can of logging paint. Since it was around 4:30 p.m., and it would be too dark to finish the layout of a cutblock today, I turned for home on another route.

On the way, I thought that this isn't so bad, and maybe I should finish all their cutblocks down here before I quit. Do you remember what happened when I had similar thoughts at Miller Western, on the day I had said I would leave?

They say *lightning* doesn't strike in the same place twice, well I got news for you, it may not look the same or be the same place, but it will still get your attention in the same way.

Right after I had those thoughts, the second drive belt burned out on the machine. You know, sometimes it's frustrating to realize that someone is listening in to your thoughts when that happens.

It was around 4:45 p.m., by then, so the only thing I could do was start walking as the snow was coming down heavier. Fortunately, I had a cut line to follow back "up" towards the truck, and I mean up, as the truck was over several hills now since I was right down beside the Brazeau River, and the truck was up on the flats, 9.6 kilometres (6 miles) away.

On the walk out, I had passed several fresh elk beds along the way, and I had that inner voice telling me that I should tell Ted that he could get a bull elk down here. I argued with that inner voice for most of the way back as I didn't want to make a promise like that and have it "fail." On the other hand, maybe God had let me come down here so that I could help Ted get a bull elk, as he would have to come back here with another machine to retrieve the double-track machine anyway.

On the way back, I had lots of time to think and talk to God. I realized I had put myself in this mess because I wasn't trusting again, that God could provide for my family. It's a familiar theme with me in case you haven't noticed. I decided right then, as I trudged up hills in the heavy snowstorm and the dark, that I would come back in to help Ted retrieve the machine, layout the three adjacent cutblocks at the bottom, and quit for good this time.

I had walked a total of 16.5 kilometres (10.3 miles) in deep snow that day. I was soaking wet with sweat by the time I got to the truck, despite the blowing snow and the -15 degrees Celsius (5°F) temperature. My legs were like "jelly" by then after going up those hills without stopping, and I started to stiffen up in the cold as soon as I stopped at the truck.

Something I discovered when I was an overweight teenager, was that, if you walked to a rhythm in your mind and kept up the cadence you could go great distances at speed, as you weren't thinking about the pain in your legs or your lungs burning for air. If you find yourself in a situation where you have a long walk you need to undertake, and it's under challenging conditions, but you can't afford to stop and rest due to the weather or the schedule, then try it. Find a song you like and keep repeating a stanza or two and walk and breathe to the beat, it will get you there. It is a valuable thing to know if you get stranded in bad weather.

The guys in the army figured this out centuries ago, and I learned it by accident when continually lagging behind the rest of the forestry class in grade 10 or 11, on winter excursions. They would stop and wait for me to catch up, but then leave as soon as I caught up, giving me no time to rest. Suddenly a 70s rock song was playing in my head, and I started to walk to the beat and noticed that I wasn't as tired while doing this.

By the time we covered the last two miles, I had caught up and passed the group, including the instructor, and arrived at the trucks ahead of them all. It was a learning experience that I believe was the result of *divine intervention* at the time, even though I hadn't recognized the source back then. It has served me very well, many times over the decades, in critical situations, and it will not fail you either. Try it!

I made it back to Ted's place around 10:30 p.m. and found them still up. Sitting down at their kitchen table to a cup of hot tea, he asked me how it went. I smiled and pulled out the burned-up drive belt and set it on the table. His eyes went wide, and he asked if I had found the old one and put it on, okay? I said, *"You mean this belt!"* and set it down on the table beside the other one.

"Oh," he said. "I guess you did, how far was the walk?"

I said, "Six miles and another four-point three miles round trip through the bush, to get tools from a feller buncher working to the northwest."

He nodded and said, *"Right, the tools,"* then smiled and shook his head and offered me another cup of tea.

As we chatted, I had that inner voice prompting me to tell Ted about the elk and that he would get one. I was hesitant to make a promise like this and tie it to God if we failed. I thought it might reinforce any negative opinion of God and church in general, but the urging was strong, so I went ahead anyway. I told him that I had come across lots of elk sign, and I believed that if he came back with me that he would get a chance at an elk. I also added that I had prayed that God would give him a shot at one.

Okay, so Ted wasn't what you might call a religious guy at all. He didn't go to any church as far as I knew, and I'm not sure he ever had. But Ted was a genuinely decent, honest, and caring person, and that meant a lot to God and me. I don't consider myself a *religious* person either, as that term, to me, indicates primarily "following a set of rules and practices that are designed to control people." Having a one-on-one relationship with God is something different, then just following the rules.

Of course, there have to be certain doctrinal precepts and practices in every denomination that identifies their adherents to that faith; otherwise, every service would devolve into anarchy. Then as long as a person does not rely on simply following those rules as the complete basis, for their relationship with God.

In my personal opinion, and if you add a couple of dollars to it, it's worth maybe a cup of coffee. If being religious is just believing what someone else has told you to do, and following their rules to fit in, then I would rather be spiritual. To me being spiritual is to know what you believe in, because you've experienced it yourself. However, not every person who claims they are spiritual has had a personal relationship with God either.

They are often still believing in someone else's experience, feeding off their energy and tagging along with them, be it a guru or a person who claims to be an enlightened master, or even some evangelists, pastors, or priests. Those life stories may give you inspiration and hope, but the only real experience that counts is the one you have yourself, and you will have them if you ask for them. You most likely already have experienced *divine intervention*, but you might not have been aware of it at the time or understood where it originated.

I don't believe in God because of someone else's opinion, written scriptures, or religious dogma. Those are valuable instructional guidelines and necessary to help a believer form a basis for their understanding of the faith. However, I believe because of personal experience and to me, that's what being a Christian should be about, but that's just my opinion. I believe that every genuine leader in any religion would, or should, want their people to have a personal experience with God, and not just hang onto the coattails of the clergy and follow the rules to keep them in-line.

By the way, to find out what happened after this trip, you'd need to follow the story in my second book: '*If Divine Intervention is Real, Do Hunters Experience It?*' as I've kept my hunting adventures out of this book. I've done this because some people might not be interested in hunting and may not understand how significant and miraculous those events of *divine intervention* were when it occurs in the field.

# CHAPTER SEVENTEEN

# Always a New Start

A month after this event took place as I was praying for a new direction, it came to my mind that I should try and contact the Ministry of Forests in British Columbia to see if they were conducting any forest inventory mapping programs. After a telephone call to their main office, I was directed to one individual who filled me in on their inventory program, which had just been underway for a couple of years. I told him who I was and my background with the Alberta Forest Inventories, and he said they hoped they could get some of Alberta's photo interpreters to work on their inventory. He sent me a stack of aerial photographs to delineate as a sample to see if I could differentiate their forest cover, and the rest is another story.

After passing their preliminary tests as well as finishing their training and passing their exam in record time, and acing it, I was allowed to bid on B.C. Vegetation Inventory contracts. It was just three months after quitting that job laying out cutblocks and doing regeneration surveys for the lumber mill in Edson, Alberta, where I wasn't supposed to be in the first place.

I contacted Jim P. and convinced him to come with me to work on the B.C. Inventory Program, and he, too, went through their training process and aced their exams with flying colours. On my way back to Alberta from Provincial Forest Headquarters in B.C., I had stopped into the Ministry of Forests office in Kamloops to ask about their inventory programs. Their Forester in charge told me that if anyone bid too low, they would reject the bid, thinking that the contractor didn't know what they were getting themselves into. So, it would make bidding a little tricky for us as we didn't know what other contractors had won their bids for in the last couple of years, and no one would tell us.

In a last-minute telephone call from the Ministry of Forest Headquarters in B.C., in March, I was informed that I would be able to bid on a contract coming up in Williams Lake, B.C. I say last minute—because the viewing would take place the next day, on Thursday, and this was

Wednesday morning and we were both still in Alberta.

So very early Thursday morning, I drove the nine hours to Williams Lake, and Jim flew in, and I picked him up at their local airport. We made it to the Williams Lake Forest Headquarters at the very end of the day, and all the other contractors had already left. We looked at the proposal, and while we were there, some B.C. companies called their office to ask if the Alberta guy had shown up.

They were worried, and they should have been. We had some inkling as to what other past inventories in southern B.C. had cost after some phone calls. Although the forest cover was very different and more complex down there, it still gave us a bit of an idea of what they were charging, well kind-of. In our opinion, they were committing "highway robbery" with their prices, and that was probably why the completion schedule for the provincial forest inventory was way behind their anticipated timeline. It was pretty clear that all the current inventory companies were in it together, to milk the province for as long as they could for as much as they could.

I'm not opposed to making a good income, but some of their pricing was ridiculous, not to mention how slow they were at their work. At the Williams Lake Forestry Office, we looked at the aerial photography and the mapping area, which extended from Alexis Creek to Nimpo Lake in the Chilcotin region. It was mostly gently rolling terrain covered in pine. We accounted for the number of field plots per map required and then figured out the helicopter time we needed. Then Jim and I sat down in the hotel room to come up with a price. Once we did finalize a price, I mentioned to Jim the *warning* I had received about being too cheap. The only problem was that we didn't know what anyone else would bid on a contract in this forest, because it was a straightforward area, species wise, so what do we put down?

We prayed about it, and that inner voice said to me, *"Double the price!"* This spiritual guidance was unnerving, as that would be twice what we could have done it for in Alberta, even though their map sheets were a bit larger. What if it was too much, and we lost the bid? But what if we bid too low and it got rejected? However, I had just undergone several instances that could only be described as *divine intervention* even to get us here, so what do I do? What would you do? Trust your wisdom, or go with what you believed was *divine intervention*?

After some consternation, I conceded to that inner voice, and I mentioned to Jim that I think we should double it. That was a risk, but we had no other guidance to go on at this point. So that's what we did! We wrote up the proposal that night and delivered it the next day to their office, and then Jim and I headed back to Alberta, on Friday afternoon, in my Isuzu Trooper in a blizzard.

It was snowing so heavy through the mountains between Prince George, B.C., and Jasper, Alberta, which all semi-trucks were pulled off to the side of the road to wait it out, but we kept going. Just as it was getting so bad in the whiteout that we couldn't distinguish the road surface from the ditch, another vehicle passed us, a Chrysler caravan of all things. That's only a two-wheel-drive vehicle, and yet it was moving much faster than we were, even though I was doing about 70 kilometres per hour (44 mph) and could barely see the road. It also had much brighter headlights than we did for some reason, so we followed its tail lights and could see the road ahead just by the illumination of its headlights. The snow was coming down so heavy, and the caravan was going so fast, that the tracks from the caravan were disappearing. And yet we could still catch a glimpse of the red tail lights ahead of us and tried to stay up with it, and we made it through the mountains.

I often wondered what *maniac* was driving that caravan through that blizzard and why it just happened to pass us and then slowed down enough for us to follow it through the worst of the storm for about 120 kilometres (72 miles). Then it sped up and was gone, and we never caught up to it after that. I must check if my guardian angel has a driver's license when we finally meet.

The next Tuesday, I got a phone call telling me that we had won the bid and that it had been 17 percent below the next highest bid, from a company that had bid 25 percent below their lowest bid ever. So, we had bid double and blew them all out of the water. What would have happened if I hadn't listened to that inner voice telling me to double the bid? Our efforts would have been for nothing. We wouldn't have been able to acquire our first contract in B.C. and would have had to wait six months to a year before more contracts came available.

Partway through that contract, there was another RFP (Request for Proposals) in the Williams Lake Forest, and we got invited to come and bid on that as well. It was east of Williams Lake and extended from south of Horsefly to north of Likely, B.C. It took in the entire Quesnel Lake area and up into the mountains to the east of there. It was a far more complex region, and although we were still working on the Chilcotin contract, we didn't want to let this one go.

I gave the rest of the Chilcotin contract to Jim to finish, and I bid on the new contract to the east of Williams Lake and won it as well. After that contract and all the auditing that they conducted, I could bid on anything in the province. They did extensive field audits to determine if my work was accurate since I was doing as much as three to four photo classifiers from other companies. Their checks verified the quality of the work, and after that, different forest regions were asking if I would come and bid on their contracts.

In some years, I would bid on all five RFPs that were available and win four of them. I would get a phone call from the Ministry's head office, asking if I could give two of them back to spread the workaround, which I gladly did. The province had a rating system with points allotted for quality, accuracy, speed of delivery, cost-effectiveness, and ease of contract relations. There were 23 other B.C. companies who all had from four interpreters to over a dozen. The rating was out of a total of 56 possible points. My ranking was 54, the highest and most sought-after company to work within the province, and I was a one-person operation. Tell me that wasn't an act of *divine intervention*!

However, the other companies started to put pressure on the government that we weren't from B.C. and taking B.C. contracts away from local companies. So, one day, I was called by the Director for the Ministry of Forests for B.C. and asked if I could move into the province. Indeed, I was willing to comply. This action would reduce pressure on the Ministry as they had given us so much work. But where do we move?

Searching for a place to move to, my family and I went on a tour within the province. We would bump into random people who always seemed to make some comment about Smithers. B.C., and the Bulkley Valley, and how nice it was there. After a while, we began to realize that through *divine intervention,* we should consider it the place to move to.

And even though three other forest regions had contacted me and asked if I would consider moving into their area and bid exclusively on their contracts. We thought we should look at Smithers, B.C. Even the people who came to give us an offer on our home south of Whitecourt, Alberta, had friends in Smithers and commented how nice it was there. How's that for coincidence, or was it?

# CHAPTER EIGHTEEN

# Prevented from a Serious Mistake

Sometimes *divine intervention* occurs to prevent you from making a grave mistake. It doesn't mean that it will stop you altogether, as you still have free will. But by putting up a roadblock and having your plans fail, it is trying to give a chance to rethink your actions and make the right decision yourself.

You can either get angry at God because nothing is working out, or take the hint and realize that it was a wrong course of action in the first place, and change your direction. Of course, you might not know what you are being saved from, as you haven't experienced it, and that will go in one of two ways for you. You will accept it and walk away, never to try it again. Or you will push forward and keep trying until you put yourself into a situation that you cannot get out of, and then see the reason why you had roadblocks to prevent you in the past. Usually, because your world has collapsed around you, you will wish you could go back and make a different decision so that you don't have to bear the consequences of your actions that put you where you ended up.

Often, in part, *divine intervention* will be to use friends or family to try and discourage you from your current path. They will try and give you advice that would detract from your intended goal, even if they don't know what you need to do. Being willing to accept that advice comes down to where your ego and trust is at, at the time. Can you trust God to take care of you anyway, if you don't go this route? Or is your pride and ego so high that you think nothing can touch you? Do you feel you are so intelligent that you think you can get out of any situation, so much so that you will probably not even consider what would happen if you failed?

That is the lie you tell yourself that allows you to forge ahead, despite all the warnings, content in your wisdom that you have it all under control. And when it falls apart, you have lost it all, and then have no place else to turn, to break free of the consequences. The emergency rooms, prisons, and morgues are full of people who ignored the advice of others, and the attempts of *divine intervention* which would have set them on a different path, and allowed them to continue to live their lives and learn their lessons in a less painful way.

I have been in situations just like that with a friend who thought they had to take the steps they were planning to succeed, and all the while, I was praying to God to put up a roadblock that they can't ignore, and save them from themselves. But if they push ahead on their own, and they did, it was just a question of time before they'd have to learn the hard way, and unfortunately, they have.

In my situation, I was also on a path that most likely would have ended in total disaster, but I thought I could handle it. Despite the urging of friends and family, I was going to do it anyway because I could formulate a reasonable argument why it was necessary, and how I could manage to carry it off.

While I was managing very successful B.C. inventory contracts, I was also paying a great deal of my contract funds on helicopter charters conducting air calls. What that would entail is a flyby at from about 100–200 metres (109–218 yards) above a stand of timber. I would make aerial assessments of the height, species composition, age, density, and understories of predetermined locations of forest stands I had chosen on the aerial photography. Sometimes the helicopter costs turned out to be almost a third of my contract budget, and I was always looking for a better deal from the helicopter companies to cut costs.

I had always wanted to fly and had spent time behind the stick, on helicopters while flying, but had never taken lessons. At about that time, there was a company out of Ponoka, Alberta, that was introducing a fully enclosed side by side two seat gyrocopter, called the RAF 2000. It had full analog instruments and cabin heat and seemed to be a capable two-seat aircraft to fly.

I thought that if I used the gyrocopter for the air calls and a helicopter for all the landings for the remote ground data collection, I would still save $40,000 to $60,000 per contract. Of course, I couldn't fly and also use my hands to hold the aerial photography and write down the air calls on the photos with a grease pencil, so my eldest son would come with me and do the writing, as I made the air call estimates while flying.

The RAF 2000 came in a homebuilt kit, of course, so I had to pick up a large box of parts and proceed to put it all together. I built most of it in only a couple of months but was having constant problems with a few simple components. The molded plastic double seat, which was also the fuel tank, would not fit into the slot well enough for me to connect the locking bolt in the very bottom, and I couldn't figure out why. Also, the electronics package was giving me problems to hook it up. It was a plug and play arrangement, but still, I couldn't get it to function correctly.

But I was determined, so I loaded the gyro onto a trailer and hauled it to Ponoka, Alberta, where they manufactured them and paid them to do the final installation. Then I needed flight training, and they agreed to do that for an hourly rate.

I had several apprehensive thoughts about using a gyro, especially in the mountains, with unpredictable winds and having to be so close to the ground. Still, I convinced myself that it would be okay. I could handle it and think of all the money I would save.

Even when I shared this with friends or family, they always asked if I thought that was going to be a good idea, to which I assured them it would be fine.

I was all set, and the gyro, which had a 120 horsepower Suzuki car engine, ran smoothly and had lots of power for the very light airframe. If I could get in enough hours of flight training, I could use it on my next contract east of Williams Lake, surrounding Quesnel Lake, B.C., and the mountains east of there for conducting my air calls.

I started the flight training, and all seemed to be going well, despite continued doubts expressed by the people I knew, and then all of a sudden, it stopped. The owner of the company who was doing the flight training, but wasn't a certified flight instructor, was told that someone from Transport Canada was snooping around the airport, and they were afraid they might lose their operating license.

All they had was suspicion and nothing else, yet it stopped my training, and I was left high and dry with no way to get enough instruction to solo on my own. I was really upset as now I had a wholly built gyroplane, but there were no instructors in Alberta to train me. I would need to conduct my air calls and ground calls on that contract with a helicopter.

However, I was fortunate enough to locate a Bell 47 Soloy from Northern Helicopters to charter for the duration of the contract. It looks like a regular Bell 47 that you might have seen in the television series *M*A*S*H* (an acronym for Mobile Army Surgical Hospital) from the 70s. But it has a conversion to a jet turbine engine with a considerable amount of additional power, compared to its original piston engine. The real benefit was that it was $200 an hour cheaper than a Bell 206 Jet Ranger, which I would typically have chartered.

Even with all that extra power, we found that we had difficulty in some locations as the working altitudes were quite high. We would also hit violent crosswinds that would tax every bit of the helicopter's ability to keep us from smacking into the mountainside.

I realized then that if I had tried to use the gyro to conduct field data collection of air calls in this location, my son Justin and I would not have survived. We would have most definitely crashed into the forest somewhere, or against a rock face, and it was all for saving a bit of money, that was already accounted for in the budget. Was that all our lives were worth, to my family or me, extra profit?

A year later, and before we had to move to B.C., which is another story, I sold the gyro for quite a loss as I didn't want to tempt fate to use it for fieldwork in the mountains if I had taken it with us. I know many would say, "You should have just kept it and flew it for fun." But I knew myself, and that I would have used it if I thought it was safe enough. And eventually, I won an inventory mapping contract right in the Bulkley Valley where I was living after the move, and sure enough, I would have tried to use the gyro, and taken the risk. Sometimes it's wiser to remove the temptation from your presence than to tell yourself that you can ignore it. But of course, you know yourself, and I don't. I'm just telling you what was best for me.

I now look at that situation at the airport in Ponoka in a different light. Realizing that it was *divine intervention* that stopped the training because I was pushing forward to where I would be in a dangerous situation. I could not have gotten out of a perilous situation flying in the mountains, and it would have cost me everything.

Sometimes you can only recognize *divine intervention* when looking back, from many years later. At least I was able to look back and learn from this event. Many don't have that luxury.

What situations have you pushed forward on, thinking you have it all under control, and yet there was an inner voice that kept warning you to turn back? That this wasn't a good idea, and that you were taking a risk you didn't need to. Did you pass it off as just being your fears that you have to push forward to overcome? Did you ignore the advice of others because you assumed, they didn't know what they were saying? Did you regret it later?

Or were you fortunate enough to listen to the guidance from your inner voice, which was your guardian angel trying to prevent you from making a drastic error in judgement? If you had listened, then you may not have then had to experience the results of total failure. But then there are things in life that we can either learn the easy way or the hard way. We don't always have to learn the hard way, as it can leave scars on ourselves and others that we can never heal. And then all the wishing in the world that you could do to change it won't help.

So, I encourage you to be sensitive to that inner voice and not let your pride and ego get the better of you and lead you down a path that will lead to a lifetime of regrets and a lot of sadness and broken hearts. This advice can be applied to many situations in life, such as finances, investing, illegal activities, or even just our relationships with people we love. The harm that comes out of choosing to satisfy your ego by telling yourself that you deserve this, and ignoring the warnings that your friends, family, or the circumstances presented to you through *divine intervention,* is never worth it.

# CHAPTER NINETEEN

# Out of the Mouth of a Child

Having been asked to move to B.C. by the Ministry of Forests to take part in their Vegetation Mapping Program, and felt we were supposed to move to the Bulkley Valley, I had contacted some real estate companies in the area. They sent me some listings of places to look at, and we raced out there to see if the place we picked suited us. We got there the night before, which is what I wanted to do so that we could look at the areas without the real estate agent with us.

One of the best places they had sent information about, that we liked was in Telkwa. It was on the west side of the Bulkley River, just 14 kilometres (9 miles) south of Smithers, and it looked lovely in the photos. It was a beautiful and large log home, right on the river for salmon fishing, and I wondered why the price was so low.

As we sat there in our vehicle admiring the property, all of a sudden, we could feel this rumble or vibration starting, and we looked at each other, somewhat puzzled. The sound got louder and louder; then the freight train whistle sounded. It passed less than 70 metres (76 yards) away just up the bank, and behind the trees, as apparently it was approaching the crossing at Telkwa. It was entirely out of sight from the front yard, but now I knew why the price was so low. If that train hadn't passed by, while we viewed the property, as it only comes by two to three times a day, apparently, we probably would have put a deposit down on the house. Then we'd have found out later, after we moved in, what a mistake we'd made. That was perfect timing, and precisely what *divine intervention* is all about.

We looked at some other properties with the agent, but nothing seemed to impress us, and then just asked for the rest of their listings to look through by ourselves. We had almost given up when we were travelling west of Telkwa on Coalmine Road and then turned south on Skillhorn Road, just wandering around. It was interesting to us; in that it was the only straight north-south road we had seen in the valley. Then near the south end of it, there was a straight road heading east called Jackpine Road, just like the grid roads on the prairies, and we stopped at the last house on the left, before a fenced pasture.

There was no 'For Sale' sign on the property, so we turned around to leave, and then our youngest son, who was about four years old, said … *"I wanna live there."*

I said, "It doesn't look like it's for sale," but something about it did seem familiar.

He said, "That's the house we're gonna live in." Okay, this is a little different, I thought, and as we sat there, we started to look through the old real estate flyers we had and found that it used to be for sale, but now the real estate sign was gone, so I thought maybe it had recently sold.

We went back into town and chatted with the real estate agent, who said that it was just recently taken off the market, as it had no offers for quite a while. We asked if we could see it anyway, and she made the arrangements. So long story short that turned out to be our new home for the next five years, while I worked on contracts all over the province of B.C. making a respectable income.

It allowed me to buy things I could never have been able to afford before and make my work more feasible. The field data collection was a large part of my contracts and now more accessible with these vehicles such as two Polaris 4x4

ATV's, Metzler inflatable boat, new 4x4 Chev extended cab 3/4-ton truck, and a 19-foot jet boat. I also was able to purchase a newly rebuilt Stinson 108-3 single-engine airplane on 2425 EDO floats that was a dream of mine to learn to fly. I bought it all for cash, I might add. I will tell you about flying in another story, but I just wanted to say that none of this would have happened if I hadn't been willing to listen to the guidance being given to me so many times by God through *divine intervention.*

What things are waiting for you to experience in life if you will finally give in to the guidance that God is more than willing to provide? Or listen to that inner voice coming from your guardian angel or whatever you feel comfortable calling it? Wherever it comes from, it doesn't have an ego! It will never reject anyone for not using the right terminology when addressing it, or for not performing some physical act. It is looking at the desires of your heart, not just listening to the words of your mouth, which are often only broadcast for others to hear, to laud praise upon yourself, and not for God alone to listen to.

# CHAPTER TWENTY

# Time to Solo

When I was in my teenage years, my dad had a desire to learn how to fly since he had been given a ride in a Cessna aircraft on occasion by the owner of the road construction company where he was employed. Whenever he would gather up enough money, he would drive two hours to the nearest flight school in Yorkton, Saskatchewan, to take lessons. Once every month for almost a year, he'd make the 360-kilometre (225-mile) round-trip to complete his ground school and flight training, and eventually got his private pilot's license.

It was a proud moment for a man who only had a grade four education and was in his late 30s. My dad had bought into a share of a small fixed-wing aircraft with two other local pilots. It was an old Stinson 108 on skis or wheels that flew out of a hangar at the airport northeast of Swan River, Manitoba. I was able to fly with him a couple of times, and it had spurred a longing in me to have my own airplane someday.

While living in Telkwa and about 34 years old, I finally had enough spare money to afford the training and hoped to get my airplane. There was a local flight school that had a gal named Sue as the trainer. I didn't have time to attend their ground school classes, and so I ordered the books and took the ground school training on my own. Then I just went in and passed the tests to qualify for the flight training. Of course, flying was not a new concept to me since I had already spent around 3,000 hours in a variety of helicopters while conducting fieldwork as well as on forest fires in Alberta. Some of that time was at the controls, as I'd ask the pilots to bring along their dual controls. But I'd never landed or taken off in a helicopter, that's for sure. No pilot would be so naïve as to risk that, but I had quite a few hours in actual flight in Jet Rangers.

The flight school out of the Smithers Airport had a Cessna 172 for students to train in, and after the first circuit, she told me to take the control yoke and land. She had an awful lot more confidence in my abilities than I did. I had doubted every time I flew, as to if this risk was worth it or not. I had a family to support, a business to run that could not continue if I wasn't healthy enough to do the work. Yet here I was trying to experience something I had desired since being a teenager when I had no responsibilities.

However, she was an excellent instructor and had quick reflexes, which came in handy at that airport. At times, violent crosswinds were coming off Hudson Bay Mountain at the Smithers Airport that, on one occasion, caught the left-wing on touchdown and tilted the plane over to the right so far that the right-wing almost touched the ground. It was one of those moments that could be re-enacted for an adult diaper commercial, although it happened so fast there wouldn't have been time for a quick photograph. That airport has peculiar winds, and on some days, the windsock at each end of the landing strip was pointing towards each other, making it especially tricky to do a *touch-and-go*.

I would fly about an hour each day with her, doing circuits and some stalls and spin recovery, which I'll admit I did not like. I have never been a thrill-seeker; despite the stories you might read about in my other book, that involved *divine intervention* and hunting, it just wasn't part of my character. I was a practical person who forced himself to do uncomfortable things only when it was necessary. Those occasions were either for someone else or to provide for my family, and this flight training was putting me and my family's future at risk for my benefit, and it seemed out of place for me.

After three hours of flight training, I was contemplating the sanity of my decision to continue and was talking to God about it. I also spoke to my wife, and she said, "If it is something you've always wanted, then you should just trust it will be okay and continue." I don't know if that gave me any comfort at the time, as I was probably looking for any good excuse to quit.

Virtually everything I had done to date was for my family. I had continuously risked injury in extremely adverse and uncomfortable conditions to provide for them. Conducting field data collection by myself in remote areas in winter, in temperatures of -40 degrees Celsius, (-40°F) for weeks on end, miles from any road, and in deep snow with no way to call for help. Being stalked by bears and having to use my Ruger Redhawk .44 Magnum with 240-grain solids to ensure I got home. Seasoned shooters will understand that using FMJ solid rounds will give three times the penetration as soft lead, and break bone more efficiently, which is the only way to end a bear attack in a hurry.

By the way, I had a rare Canadian permit to carry my .44 Mag or my Glock .40 caliber, while working in remote locations. So, it was legal (trust me those are very hard to acquire under Canadian gun laws). I was always working solo in the early years before my eldest son joined me at the age of about 11 to hang ribbons on the route into the field plots. This flight training was the first thing I was doing that was basically for me. So, after some soul searching, I went back again the next day to continue my training.

That became an exhilarating day in that my flight instructor and I did two circuits, and then after landing the second time and moving over to a taxiway and stopping the aircraft at her request, she got out.

She then turned around while standing in the open doorway and said, "Okay, it's all yours."

My only response was, "What?"

She said, "It's time to solo; you can do it, then bring it to the hangar after you land."

Have you ever had a *pucker* moment (military slang phrase) in your life where fear grips your chest so tight that it becomes hard to breathe? Well, I had one of those moments. Now, if I'd been a thrill-seeker, I would have been ecstatic that I could solo after only 3.5 hours of flight training in a Cessna 172.

But I wasn't the kind of person who goes skiing in the mountains, rock climbing, racing motorcycles, or surfing (well I can't swim, so that was out for sure). And certainly not like the thrill-seekers of today that fill the hospital emergency wards every single week, while trying to get that perfect video for YouTube. Despite the many situations where I was in dangerous circumstances, due to the elements or from predatory wildlife, none of them were by choice. This one would be by choice, and only one small mistake on landing would get me into the newspaper, and not in the best way.

The thought briefly ran through my head that she's trying to get me killed, but that was silly as we had a good relationship, and I only paid by the hour, so there was no benefit in that approach. It is strange what thoughts attack you in a moment of stress and anxiety, though, isn't it? I have to say that I was praying the whole time from the take-off leg and climbing to altitude for the circuit, then turning crosswind to the west of the airport, and later on the downwind leg and then the turning east on the base leg. I was so tense that I would have exploded before I could pass wind, and then a strange thing happened. On the final leg, just before touchdown, I gave it all to God and said, "Lord, whatever is supposed to happen, it is okay with me," and I meant it. Suddenly all the tension left me, and I relaxed just before my wheels touched down, and it was a perfect landing.

Giving up control of the outcome means a total surrender to a power that is far greater than I, and with everything God had brought me through and done for me, I knew he was working on my behalf. If this were my time to roll that piece of aluminum up into a ball, and they would have to use a can opener to cut me out of it, then that was out of my hands. *Fear* is both useful (in that it can keep you out of trouble and keep you safe) and harmful (in that it can keep you from experiencing growth and learning to trust). I'll admit it's tough to know the difference some times.

After that, flying solo did not create the anxiety that once had gripped me. As training continued, we flew all over the region, and into every small airstrip we could find, from Stewart, B.C. on the west coast to Fort Fraser, in the interior. I even landed in the rocky pasture out in front of our home on Jackpine Road.

During my flight training, I started to search for an aircraft to buy and found a rebuilt Stinson 108-3 in Ontario. It had a brand new 235 horsepower continental engine on 2425 EDO floats with an 82-inch variable pitch prop. It got upgraded from a 175 horsepower Franklin engine and a 76-inch prop and was now referred to as a Super Stinson. I bought the plane, and the owner flew it out and landed at Tyhee Lake just north of

Telkwa, where about 26 floatplanes docked around the shoreline.

During my ground school exam, I noticed that the airplane example they would use was that; you were flying aircraft CF-ABC from Point A to Point B, etcetera. When my time with the flight examiner came around, I asked him if they knew that there was an aircraft with the same designation, they used in all their standardized tests, and he said, "No, there isn't; that's why they use it?" At which point, I pulled out a picture of my new Super Stinson and showed him the call sign: CF-ABC. Now isn't that a coincidence?

Sometimes God has a sense of humour in fulfilling our wishes and does things so unique that it can't be a pure coincidence. But when *divine intervention* is needed, as in my first solo landing, the spirit is close by to give comfort and to calm your fears when it's needed. Our only task is to learn to trust, and that often means we require exposure to uncomfortable situations, but it's the only way to grow as a person and become more than what we imagined we could be.

# CHAPTER TWENTY-ONE

# Oil on the Windshield

I had completed my flight training, or so I thought, and they had scheduled a flight examiner to come up to Smithers to test the new prospective pilots. I took my test and although I didn't ace it, who cares! I passed. But a few days later, my flight trainer, Sue, told me that they couldn't issue my license as I didn't have enough flight hours.

I needed 40 hours of flight training to earn a Canadian license, and I only had 35.5 logged, even though 32 of those hours were PIC or solo. She said I had to do a cross-country solo as well before they would authorize the license. I was heading out to conduct field data collection on an inventory mapping project on Vancouver Island in another two days, and wouldn't be back for weeks, so I had to do this right now, and the standard one hour per day wouldn't suffice.

So, I planned to fly all 4.5 hours off in one day by completing two extended cross-country flight plans. I would take off from Smithers Airport, fly south to Houston, B.C., then east cross-country to Fort Saint James and land at their little airstrip.

I would then take off again and head to Vanderhoof, B.C., for a flyover of the airport, then to Fort Fraser airstrip, and then back to Houston before landing at Smithers to fuel up. If you have a look on Google Earth, you will see that it's a distance of around 500 kilometres (312 miles) cross-country. I would then fuel up and fly from Smithers to Telkwa, then turn west and go through the narrow Telkwa Pass, with peaks 2,200 metres high (7,300 feet) and 2,500 metres (8,200 feet) on either side of the pass. Earlier that year, it had claimed the lives of three pilots who slammed into the wall while flying in low cloud in a Twin Otter, as they were flying it back to the prairies from southern Alaska after purchasing it.

Then I'd cross the coastal mountains to Kitimat, B.C., make a swing out over the ocean and approach the Kitimat Airport from the south, and do a *touch-and-go*. I'd then head up to Terrace, B.C., and, after that, follow the highway to the northeast travelling past Kitwanga, then Hazelton, and finally back to the airport at Smithers. That's another 400 kilometres (250 air miles). All in all, it would give me just over 5.5 hours in the air on a 6.5-hour flight day. It'd be a long day, but I was used to being in the air for 10- to 12-hour days in helicopters for weeks on end, so this wasn't a stretch, I thought. But sometimes things don't go as planned.

I took off from Smithers and made the first three legs okay and was on my way back to Houston, B.C., when I noticed something strange on the windshield. By the way, that's never a good thing when you're flying a small plane. I had a line of oil working its way up the windshield in front of me, and it was a bit concerning too say the least. Of course, you can't just pull over and have a look under the hood when you're flying, right! By the time I reached Smithers, I had three small lines of oil running from the bottom to the top of the windshield. As they refueled the airplane, I radioed the flight training school to have a mechanic come out and take a look, which they did.

Sue was there as well, and the verdict from the mechanic was that it was probably just some spilled oil from the recent oil change, and I needn't worry. Okay, that didn't exactly give me a lot of confidence, but I had to finish the last flight plan, so I took off again and headed south towards Telkwa and then swung west towards the gap that was the Telkwa Pass.

As I approached the Pass, a couple of miles back at about 1,830 metres (6,000 feet) above sea level, the plane engine *coughed*. Now I don't know if you've ever been flying a small single-engine aircraft, which had just experienced oil leaking from the engine in the previous hour. But if you are then heading towards a narrow mountain pass, and the engine coughs, and the plane shudders like it did at that moment, it gets your immediate attention. That would have been another perfect time to test the efficiency of an adult diaper.

But that was all that happened, and I continued listening intently for any more anomalies coming from the engine. There weren't any, but despite the feeling that I should turn back, I kept going towards the Telkwa Pass, which I was rapidly approaching. Once I went through that pass, there was no place to land a Cessna 172 on wheels until I got to Kitimat, 83 kilometres (52 miles) away. Also, once you go through the Pass, and scan the horizon, it's very unnerving as all the mountain peaks look the same, one after another for as far as the eye can see. There are no roads, no lakes, nothing to get your bearings except snow-capped mountains, one after another.

After about 20 minutes, I was relieved to see the valley up ahead towards Kitimat. I crossed the highway to the west side of the valley

and then headed south and out over the ocean inlet, and then turned north again towards the
Kitimat airstrip, just as the oil started to creep up
the windshield for a second time. I had to ask
God what was happening and why this was occurring, but I never got an answer. I headed for
the little Kitimat airstrip and lined up for a landing and realized that it was nothing but a grass
airstrip. There were no services of any kind, and
it was 13 kilometres (8 miles) north of town.

I didn't want to be stranded out there, so a
thought came to me that I wouldn't do a *touch-
and-go*. I decided that I'd fly a few feet above the
airstrip and then climb back out again and continue northward, which is what I did, as another
line of oil started to make its way up the windshield. As I headed north towards the Terrace
Airport and then turned northeast to follow the
road, the oil lines on the windshield didn't seem
to be growing, so I continued.

As I flew roughly 51 kilometres (32 miles)
northeast of Terrace, the oil started streaming up
the windshield again with new streaks accumulat-
ing, by the minute. I decided to cut my trip short
and turned directly east. By that time, I was 70
kilometres (44 air miles) across country to
Smithers and 61 kilometres (38 air miles) back to
Terrace, so I elected to head for home base as I
didn't want to be stranded in Terrace. I travelled

along the south side of the Seven Sisters Peaks, not 33 metres (100 feet) above those brilliant white glaciers. As I passed over, I contemplated my chances of survival if forced down on them, and it wasn't promising.

The mountains all looked the same again, of course, and I hadn't mapped out this leg of the route, so no one knew I was heading home on this route. But I knew where Smithers was, roughly, and I headed in that direction, hoping I would make it before the oil leaks made the engine quit. With oil covering my entire side of the windshield, so that I had to lean over to my right to see the tarmac ahead at the Smithers Regional Airport, I brought the Cessna down and taxied over to the hangar. I informed them by radio that the oil leak wasn't just from something spilled during the oil change, as my whole windshield was covered.

This revelation brought a few people out to have a look, and there were some embarrassing looks from the mechanic. Sue seemed quite worried and gave me a hug when I got out of the Cessna. On the walk into their office, she said they had tried to get me by radio, but of course, there are no facilities at Kitimat to relay a radio message and no communications over the mountains by the time I was in the Kitimat Valley. That airstrip had been declared *unserviceable* that day by Transport Canada. This notice was because of all the recent rain and the spring thaw, and it was way too soft to land on it.

If I had touched down, I would have nosed over with the Cessna and rolled it into a ball, and it would have been can opener time. With 13 kilometres (8 miles) to town, there would have been no help for quite a while, and that would have been the end of my trip, permanently.

I ask you then, what aspect of this event displayed what I might call a *divine intervention* moment? I was upset about the oil leak and the risk it put me in, simply because the mechanic had made a bad call. But I think it was preparing me to be extra concerned if it happened again. When the engine coughed before I made it to the Telkwa Pass, I think it was a gentle warning to turn back and potentially avoid a fatal accident at the Kitimat airstrip. Then the oil started to stream up the windshield again as I was approaching the airfield and that caused me to choose to do a low flyby instead of a *touch-and-go*, which would have been more like a touch and roll and crumple and flames and screaming and crying and—well you get the idea.

So, bear in mind that sometimes *divine intervention* can seem like an unwanted event and it will make you angry. However, the fact may be that it is the very act that preserved you for another day, or kept you from doing something ill-advised that would have ruined your life or a relationship that you cherish. Often, we don't recognize it at the time, and remain angry at God or the people around us and do not display any gratitude for what was a lifesaving act. Guardian angels must feel under-appreciated sometimes, and I think I'll have some apologizing to do when I meet mine.

# CHAPTER TWENTY-TWO

# Hammerhead

Sometimes a *divine intervention* can merely take the form of reminding you of something significant when you need it the most. After all, millions of ideas and memories could come to your mind at any given time, but having your memory jogged with precisely what you need, is undoubtedly better compartmentalization of thoughts than I could do on my own.

After I had that experience with the Cessna, my confidence vanished in flying that aircraft, and I never rented it again. Also, I had a newly rebuilt Super Stinson moored at Tyhee Lake at a rented spot on a private dock, so there was no need to look to the Cessna any longer.

The difficulty was, I had never flown on floats and wasn't licensed to do so. I checked around and found a commercial pilot that worked in the same building as the flight school and was certified for training on floats, so I made arrangements to pay him for the hours I needed. In Canada, we needed seven hours of flight training, including five takeoffs and landings on floats as a solo pilot to qualify for the seaplane rating.

One day, we met at where I docked my Super Stinson on Tyhee Lake, and we flew out to a small lake east of Telkwa, which was more like a puddle than a lake at only a few hundred metres long. He showed me how to land and take off, and one particularly exhilarating maneuver was to do a circular take off on one float.

The purpose of this was to gain enough speed to reach take-off velocity on a lake that was too short to do it in a straight-line run. It was tricky in that as you built up some forward momentum, you then tilted your control yoke over to the left to lift the right-wing up and raise the right float out of the water. Then you used the rudder to direct the plane to travel in a counter-clockwise circle. Okay, the choice of which wing to lift and which rudder peddle to use, to cause a clockwise or counter-clockwise take off, is dependent upon which seat you occupy—If it's tandem seating (one behind the other), it doesn't matter. But if it's side by side, then you always tilt the aircraft towards the pilot's side so you can look out and see that the wing tip never touches the water.

Of course, you realize what happens if it touches the water at 62 miles per hour, right! At the end of an hour and fifteen minutes, he had to head back to base as he had a commercial flight booking to attend to, so we returned.

He then found out that he'd be away for a few days and told me just to be careful and practice. Okay—I thought. I probably don't have to tell you that doing a solo takeoff and landing in a floatplane with just one hour of training (the last 15 minutes was ferry time back and forth from the lake) and 40 hours of total flight time before that, was a little unnerving.

My *co-pilot*, which I believe sat beside me the whole time, knew how to fly without an aircraft, during the rest of my solo flight time. After a couple of weeks, I went back to the instructor and asked to be signed off on my seaplane certification since I had around 15 hours in my logbook on floats, and I was still alive. So that's the limit of my training, and now I was off on my own.

I couldn't have picked a better aircraft to buy for the money at the time, as it was a hot rod on wings. A light fabric airplane with a 235-horsepower engine allowed me to take off with full fuel and two people on board in 13 seconds, and then climb out at a 45-degree angle. This plane would save my "bacon" on several occasions, as often lousy judgement can be overridden with a sufficient application of raw power. And in the beginning years, my decisions needed lots of raw power to keep me from becoming a statistic.

The other pilots out there, who had survived, gave me good advice when I asked. One elderly gentleman named George had parked his Stinson on wheels just outside of our property, on the pasture belonging to the rancher. He had told me a couple of years before, that every mountain pass, out there, had plane wreckage in it.

He also told me that they lose one plane and pilot from Tyhee Lake every year, and unfortunately, that was true for all the years we lived there. The coastal mountains are especially treacherous to fly in due to the powerful crosswinds coming off the ocean. They can be so strong and hit you at 160 kilometres per hour (100 mph) without warning, as you pass the face of a gap and drive you sideways towards the mountainside. If you aren't staying alert, you will make a real mess on the slope.

Also, you may be headed for a notch in the mountain to get over into the next valley, and it suddenly closes, as low cloud moves in from the other side, and you can't see daylight or even how high the pass is anymore. Some might say, *"Well, it's just a cloud, fly through it."* It works okay on the prairies, but not in the coastal mountains. A saying which emphasizes this is, *"The clouds are made of stone."* A song was written on that theme by a local artist back in the 90s after a bush pilot friend of mine, and his two children died in a fiery crash a few hours north of Smithers. We attended a few too many memorials for pilots while we lived there.

There is only one maneuver while flying in the mountains, that will keep you from appearing like someone dumped a large bucket of garbage on the rock wall, and that's called a *Hammerhead*. It was described to me by George before I ever took flying lessons, but it was not taught at the flying school years later.

The reason they don't teach it I believe, is that it violated the maximum angle of attack that was allowed by the aircraft manufacturer's flight specifications. Indeed, many an aircraft that slammed into a wall was often the result of pilots not willing to push the plane beyond the maximum angle of attack, which they had been trained to observe during training. The reason being is twofold; it might overstress the airframe, and it would undoubtedly stall the aircraft, which is a bad thing when you can already see the eyes on mountain marmots watching your last moments on this Earth. Mind you, slamming into the mountain stresses the airframe as well.

The maneuver was described to me by George, but I was never shown how to do it in the air and never practiced it, and forgot all about it as I never planned on having to execute it. You know what reality does to the best-laid plans, right!

One day I had decided that we would make a trip to the coast to try and catch some salmon and fly there in the Super Stinson. Trevor, an employee of mine, a terrific young man, and my eldest son, were accompanying me. We headed off early one morning to land on a long narrow lake on the north end of Prince Royal Island, as I had heard that salmon were coming up the river into the lake to spawn.

I wanted to take a direct route, which would lead us to a long valley that was south of the Telkwa Pass and travelled southwest until we came to the Atna Range. Crossing the range just to the right of Atna N4, which was 2,360 metres (7,729 feet) in altitude, there was a saddle that was at 2,089 metres (6,320 feet) elevation on the north side of the peak. On the other side of it was a 32-kilometre (20-mile) long valley that continued southwest to the top of the Kildala Arm, which was the east arm of the inlet that served Kitimat, B.C.

It was a lovely day for flying, but as we got right up to the Atna Range and headed for one of the few high elevation passes, there was suddenly a dense cloud that moved through the pass very quickly, coming towards us and cutting off our route. It was being pushed up that long valley by high wind and suddenly forced up the mountainside. We didn't have the altitude to climb over the taller part of the mountain or the time to gain it, and that would be foolish anyway because we could no longer see the peak. I was already in too tight, and it was too narrow to circle back the way we came. In a moment of near panic and thinking of what I could do, George's words came back to me as clear as a bell.

I quickly banked the plane over to the right side of the rapidly narrowing pass as the rock wall in front of me was approaching at 2,656 metres (2,900 yards) a minute, and I was only 275–366 metres (300–400 yards) from it. If you do the math, you'll know how long we had for this world. Okay, this isn't a math quiz, so I'll do it for you. At a speed of 2,656 metres (2,900 yards) a minute, which is 160 kilometres per hour (100 mph), it covers 44 metres (48 yards) per second. A distance of 366 metres (400 yards) is travelled in 8.3 seconds. Not much time to come up with a plan and discuss it with the passengers on board and take a vote, wouldn't you agree?

As I got close to the right side of the rock wall, I gave it full power and pulled back hard on the yoke, and the plane pointed straight up, and then I jammed my foot down on the left rudder peddle. This motion spun the plane around on the center axis like doing a flat spin, but at a 90-degree angle to the surface, I was instantly pointing downhill at a very steep angle, in roughly the center of the valley I had entered.

Trevor in the back wasn't expecting this, as I had no time to warn anyone, and he was able to revisit what he had for breakfast that morning and make use of the little bags we carry. After that, we flew a short way further to the north and went through a much lower pass that brought us out near Kitimat and then headed south onto the lake we were going to go fishing.

There will be people who will say it was only your memory recall that brought it to you, and there was no *divine intervention*. So, tell me, what brings things forward in your memory at precisely the right time, when in a crisis? Is it merely rational thought that sifts through a billion memories that have filled your mind over the past three or four years and instantly found the right file and opened it with seconds to spare, in time to take the right action?

I suppose if I had never experienced all of the unique and unexplainable circumstances in the past, where it was undeniably clear that *divine intervention* was at play in my life, I might have been skeptical also. But as I said early on, a *skeptic* is just someone with no personal experience, and only has their doubts to guide them. They then form an opinion based on a lack of evidence, instead of an abundance of evidence. In my viewpoint, that seems like a less than credible way to go through life while claiming that their opinion is valid!

# CHAPTER TWENTY-THREE

# Glassy Landing

I had many experiences in my Super Stinson floatplane in the few years that I owned it, and there was nary a trip where some life-threatening situation did not occur. I would share these experiences with people at the church, and it had a strange effect. No one wanted to fly with me! I thought that to be strange because if you had a choice, would you instead fly with someone who has gotten out of dozens of near-fatal incidents that were caused by the flying conditions in the coastal mountains while going cross-country? Or would you instead fly with someone who only flew on fair-weather days, followed highways, and had never experienced adverse conditions, ever? What do they do when they are caught off guard?

Think about it, because you can never control the weather and flight plans change involuntary. Which pilot is more mentally prepared for an emergency in the air and able to deal with it? Is it the one who has experienced many of them and survived, while local experienced pilots were dying at a rate of about one or two per year? Or would it be the pilot who has never experienced adverse conditions, because they always think they can avoid risky situations?

Or is it the one who calls for help and listens to that inner voice giving instructions when they are needed. After all, God will neither force you to listen nor force you to take instructions and act upon them. You see that *divine intervention* is only offered to you as a choice. It is always your free will to take the advice and make it through, or not to take the help, and suffer the consequences. Survival isn't a guarantee, because we have a free will to choose our actions—think about that.

I'll share two situations where unexpected natural conditions can cause a pilot to take the wrong action, and it can cause a tragic accident and how God helped me through them. One exciting trip was to Tchesinkut Lake, which is just south of Burns Lake, B.C.

The wife of Pastor Stan H. of the Christian and Missionary Alliance Church in Smithers had relatives on the north shore of the Tchesinkut Lake who ran a cattle company. Each year in the spring, they turned the cattle out into the bush to graze and would gather them up in the fall. This particular year they were missing about 40 head, and since the forest was so dense and there were no fences to keep the cattle within any distance of the ranch, they couldn't locate them. Stan asked if I could come down to help out with my plane, and of course, I was eager to do so. I arrived in the late morning and flew to the east end of the lake and made my landing approach heading west as their ranch was on the north side of the lake about halfway up the shoreline.

There wasn't even the slightest amount of wind that day and many people might think that's a good thing when landing on water, but that's a deadly situation. It causes more fatal floatplane accidents than rough water does. The reason being is what we call, a *glassy landing*. You see, a mirror-smooth water surface provides no visual clues as to where the water surface lies. Without that reference point, a pilot will believe the surface is still many feet below them and come in at too steep of an angle, and would not have flared before touchdown. The impact with the water violently flips the plane over on its nose, knocking out the pilot and passengers, and they drown, upside down in the flooded aircraft.

I was landing on a truly glassy surface that day, and as I was coming down, thinking the lake was still about 6 metres (20 feet) below me, I had not started to flare the plane back yet for the landing. Suddenly out of the corner of my right eye, I spotted a *single leaf* on the surface of the water. And my floats had to be no more than inches from the surface. An instant of panic shot through me as it seemed like the control yoke was yanked back towards me all on its own, and I shot back up about 6 metres (20 feet) and continued on my way. The realization went through me like pouring cold water down your back on a hot day that I had almost died and was just two or three seconds from doing so.

I continued around one more time, circling to the north and seeing Stan standing near the dock on the shore, and I started my landing run further back this time to do it properly. I had never landed on glassy water before but had been told about it by my flight instructor in that amazing one-hour lesson, which is all I had on floats before I was on my own to learn the hard way.

This time, I started my landing approach by flaring back on the plane, as if already on the surface, yet many feet above the water. The principle is to maintain that angle of attack, and then slowly reduce the throttle. This allows the plane to settle down on the water, with the floats at the correct angle. This way, the bow of the floats won't dig into the surface and flip you over. But of course, you cannot go below stall speed either, or you will instantly lose lift and plunge into the lake in a most spectacular fashion.

Oh, I should mention that my Super Stinson did not have a stall horn, which warns the pilot when the aircraft is about to stall, so the airspeed indicator is the only way to know if you're about to die, and that airspeed in my plane was 62 miles per hour (99 kph). I guess the benefit of having no stall horn, is that at least that way, a person doesn't have all that tension building up of a loud horn blaring, and warning of impending doom, frightening everyone, right!

If my airspeed indicator read 61 miles per hour (97.6 kph), though, you'd better be a fair distance above the surface, because you will need time to recover and gain airspeed, to avoid meeting God face to face in a premature encounter. Not that I don't want to meet God; it's just that I don't want to arrive earlier than my scheduled appointment. By the way, my old plane had analog instruments, not digital, so the airspeed indicator was just a bouncing needle on a dial.

When executed correctly, a glassy water landing is so smooth that you don't even feel that you are down on the water, and your first indication is the sound of the floats slicing through the surface at a shallow angle. Having survived the landing and not telling anyone about it, we had a bit of lunch at Stan's father-in-law's ranch house, and then he and Stan would accompany me to look for cattle in the dense bush from the air.

I flew a grid pattern back and forth over the forest at around 300 metres (1,000 feet) altitude above ground level, and since they were both on the right side of the plane, I tilted the yoke over to the right and pushed in the left rudder and flew at around 63–65 miles per hour (101–104 kph). This maneuver tilted the plane over at about a 40-degree angle to the right and allowed them to look straight down, while I still travelled in a straight line and kept the same altitude. I had never seen this done before and had no idea it could work since it certainly wasn't part of flight school training, but it should be, in my opinion.

In any search and rescue taking place in thick timber, spotters in the aircraft have to look out of the windows at a shallow angle. This angle precludes them from looking down through the trees, which in reality, is the only way you will spot someone in dense forest, as at even the slightest angle, they'll be hidden by the standing timber.

We had been up for about an hour and spotted a few cattle, and then we spotted a bull moose. Okay, this was bad for the passengers, I'll admit that. Since I had been in B.C., I had never had a decent moose hunt as the populations were particularly low in the places I had been, with nary a track anywhere, and if you've read my other book on hunting stories, you'll understand why I liked hunting bull moose.

Of course, the moose was on their side of the plane since they spotted it, but I wanted to see it. So, since the ailerons were already tilting the right-wing down at a 40-degree angle, when I kicked in the right rudder, the plane instantly pointed its nose at the ground, and we gained speed rapidly.

I spotted the moose and headed for it to have a better look, as I could see it through the front windshield since I was pointing straight down at it. I have to admit I think it must have looked pretty cool to watch a floatplane do that if you were standing on the ground, as you never see those kinds of maneuvers from an aircraft on floats. I pulled out in the last few seconds, and applied full power, clawing my way back up to altitude.

Stan was in the back seat, and I heard him on the radio headset, asking me to *"Please, not do that again!"* As I glanced back, I noticed he was holding a bag and examining his previous meal from lunch—oops, my bad! After we landed an hour or two later, his father-in-law expressed a similar sentiment to him, which he then passed on to me on the way back to Smithers, when I gave him a ride home.

But in my defense, my reaction was the result of a lifetime of hunting. And if you read my second book: '*If Divine Intervention Is Real, Do Hunters Experience It?*' which focuses on events that took place on my hunting trips. You might realize why saying "bull moose" to me while flying, is like the dogs in the 2009 animated movie by Pixar called *Up* when someone yells "squirrel!" So, in a way, this was their fault, at least that's my defense.

On the way home, Stan made the mistake of asking me what I had done to make the plane do that, so I showed him. I instantly dropped the plane to the right, and before I could point it at the ground, his weight hit the door on his side, and it popped open, as he hadn't closed it properly. Fortunately, his seat belt was on, and I flipped the plane level again and said, *"See just like that."* There's nothing like the adrenalin rush that one can have when your door pops open on a small plane while it's tilted over at 40 degrees, and you're looking straight down at the ground from 1,525 metres (5,000 feet) above ground level, to wake a person up, right? Another adult diaper commercial for sure!

However, if that single leaf hadn't been on the water exactly where I was coming down out in the middle of that lake, things would have turned out quite differently that day and for me. And as far as I know, that leaf was placed there through *divine intervention* and that control yoke snapping back against me had a little help, I believe.

# CHAPTER TWENTY-FOUR

# Downdraft

The next natural scenario that can happen without warning and as a pilot you don't even know it is happening most of the time is what's called a *downdraft*. That has slammed many pilots into the ground in a properly functioning aircraft. And it is almost always due to panic on the part of the pilot.

My eldest son and I were going moose hunting, so we loaded up the aircraft for a three-day trip and headed up to Tatlatui Lake, which is about 260 kilometres (162 air miles) north of Tyhee Lake at Telkwa, where I kept my Super Stinson. But I would fly northeast first to the top of Babine Lake and then follow the valleys and passes up to Tatlatui so it would be around 304 kilometres (190 air miles) one way.

The trip was uneventful on getting to the lake, we approached from the east and turned south into the lake and landed facing southwest into the wind. The wind was blowing at about 50 kilometres per hour (30 mph), and we had one metre (three-foot) waves and white caps on the lake as we came down to land. I don't know if you have landed in very choppy water before, but what you hear is *boom-boom-boom-boom-boom* as the floats would hit the tops of each wave set, and it, shudders the plane violently.

About two-thirds the way down the lake, there is a bit of a peninsula sticking out on the west shore. We taxied over that direction to the north side of it as it would shelter us from the wind and make it easier to tie up the plane without it being damaged against the rocks by the waves. It was calm in the tiny inlet, and we set up camp just 6 metres (20 yards) from the plane.

By the way, when you come into a shore with no dock, you come in nose first with the front of the floats touching the sand. You get out and walk along the top of the float and step off into the shallow water, to stop the momentum of the plane, so the floats don't impact hard on the rocks. After unloading, however, you push the plane out, and by holding the ropes, you guide it around so that the rear of the floats come in to touch the shore. This direction allows you to take off quickly after you have loaded the plane.

You see, with the front of the floats being deeper, they are closer to the bottom. You can inadvertently load a plane up with too much weight and not realize that your floats are stuck fast in the lake bottom because of the added weight. By turning it around, the front of the floats, which take most of the load from the plane, are out in deeper water. It makes it much easier to take off—that, and the fact that small planes don't have reverse.

We tried moose calling that evening and had one bull answer but couldn't entice him in. It was a little early for the rut and still quite warm out, so it would be slow action. But what activity we did find that was "hot and heavy," was the trout fishing. Standing near our tent the next morning after trying to call moose again with no luck, I noticed that trout were jumping continuously about 109 metres (100 yards) to the west and at the mouth of a small creek feeding the lake.

We took the fishing gear and walked over there and tried our luck off the gravel bar that was stretching out past the feeder creek, and it was terrific. Every single cast, we would catch a one-kilogram (two-pound) rainbow trout. And it didn't matter what lure we used. We took some video footage of trying any lure in the tiny tackle box and making a cast, and we'd "nail" a beautiful rainbow. After one more night there and calling for moose in the evening and the morning with no success, we decided to leave.

The weather was getting worse, and we could see tall whitecaps all over the lake and knew it would be extremely rough out there. But we had 320 metres (350 yards) of relatively calm water heading east before we hit the crosswind coming from the southwest and the tall whitecaps. And we were in a Super Stinson, which made all the difference.

We packed away the many trout we had caught, loaded up our camp gear, and headed out at full throttle and were airborne before we even hit the whitecaps. We flew north to almost the north end of Tatlatui Lake and then turned east down a valley that led to Thutage Lake. Intersecting the lake at the mid-point, we then turned right and flew down to almost the southwest end of the lake. We then turned directly south into a valley that would allow us to follow a series of valleys back to Babine Lake. By the way, you can look up all these locations on Google Earth and see where we went and how utterly remote and rugged the country is if you're inclined to do so.

As we turned south and proceeded along that valley with a mountain range to the southwest of us and a tall ridge to our right, I noticed we were losing altitude rather quickly. I opened the throttle all the way and pulled back on the yoke a little, and there was no change, and we continued to sink. I checked the airspeed, and it showed 64 miles per hour (102 kph), just barely above stall speed, and we were at full throttle, which is usually 110 miles per hour (176 kph) and flying level, or so I thought. In actuality, the plane was trying to climb as best it could, but we were heading towards the trees.

I didn't say anything to Justin as there was no point, and as I watched the ground getting closer, it all of a sudden hit me— DOWNDRAFT! We got caught in a downdraft coming over the mountains to our right and pushing us towards the surface. If we had been successful hunting and a heavily loaded plane with 270 kilograms (roughly 600 pounds) of deboned moose on board, we would never have made it.

I was trying to think of what to do as we had never trained for this in-flight school, and that inner voice said, *"Just stay level, don't fight it, and don't try and gain altitude and pull up, or you will stall and crash."* So that's what I did. I watched us getting closer and closer to the trees, and fortunately, there was a bit of a strip through the middle of the valley, that only had a low brush in it along the river. When we were no more than 18 metres (60 feet) above the ground, the sinking stopped, and we flew level and gained airspeed, then slowly started to climb back out.

The *downdraft* can't continue into the surface, of course, so it hits the ground, and then the wind is forced back up again as it climbs the slope on the opposite side of the valley. If at any point, I had tried to fight it any more than keeping power on and pulling back as far as I dared on the yoke to stay above stall speed, I would have stalled out the aircraft. Being only a very short distance above the ground already and having no time to recover from a stall, that's where they would have found the wreckage after a few days of searching when we did not return from the trip.

So, was *divine intervention* at play that day? I believe so, in that suddenly being aware of what was happening and what to do instead of panicking. You see, *divine intervention* doesn't always have to show itself in the way of dramatic action, sometimes it manifests itself in providing calm, and giving you an insight into what is going on, so a person does not panic and react in the wrong way. You can judge for yourself, of course. For me, I was thankful for being alerted to what was happening, even though there was no other physical sign of the *downdraft*, other than what my instruments were telling me.

# CHAPTER TWENTY-FIVE

# Follow Those Tail Lights

Sometimes God directs you through a dangerous situation that no sane or rationally thinking person would undertake on purpose. Or is it more likely that you head out on the journey despite the warnings from your guardian angel, and they have to work extra hard to keep you alive because you didn't do your homework? Having a relationship with a supernatural power can make up for a lot of foolish mistakes in life, but not all of them. Our free will choices can get us into things that we can't get out of, and then we have to live with the consequences.

One such trip took place when Larry M. and his son came up from Whitecourt to visit us in Telkwa, B.C. Larry was ten years older than I, and we were great friends for many years. We met after my wife and I, moved to Whitecourt from Edmonton while I worked as a Forest Ranger for the Alberta Forest Service. They lived in the same trailer court as we did, and on occasion, we had gone to the same church. Larry was a hunter, and so was I, so we had that as our primary focus on friendship as well.

I was planning to take Larry up to Dick Lake, where two friends and I had taken three caribou a couple of years before (it's in the other book folks), and hopefully, get him a caribou. We loaded the plane, and for extra fuel, I filled a few 18-litre (4-gallon) collapsible water jugs with avgas to take along so we wouldn't have to make as many stops for fuel on the trip.

Once our packs, tent, and food were loaded, the plane was pretty full. Then as an afterthought, I also loaded split blocks of firewood into the floats as there would be none where we were going. I hadn't bothered to do a weight balance calculation, unfortunately, and I believe the Super Stinson was grossly overloaded.

A second indication that it was overloaded was that it took us over a mile to get off the water, and that was certainly unusual for this aircraft. I realized then that just maybe we had too much weight on board. I guessed when I stepped on the float to get into the plane, and it sank below the waterline, that should have been my first indication, right!

I should give a warning here to seasoned pilots. You could suffer temporary whiplash while reading this story due to rapidly rolling your eyes back into your head while you consider the stupidity of my actions. And also, be cautious of dislocating your neck, from the head shaking you may also experience. Hey, I never *claimed* to be a person who followed the rules of flight safety, and I think this story might confirm it to you, so sit back and relax and be thankful you weren't flying with me that day.

After the very long surface run on Tyhee Lake, we headed north and followed Highway 16 until it started to swing west and then proceeded north cross-country on the east side of Kispiox Mountain and then northwest to meet up with Highway 37. Flying back then in an aircraft built in the late 1940s; I had no GPS instruments to guide me. So, following highways, rivers, or valleys were the only means of navigation while referencing surface features to an aeronautical flight map and following a compass.

During that stretch between Kispiox Mountain and connecting with Highway 37, I noticed a lot of patchy clouds moving in, and we were dodging them along the way. I also noticed that I was using a lot more fuel than usual, which made sense due to the extra weight we were carrying in fuel containers, firewood, and way too much gear. So much so, that by the time we got to Me-ziadin Lake on the west side of Highway 37, we were already down to half fuel. I landed out in the lake and was planning to dump some fuel into the wing tank on my side, from the four-gallon collapsible water containers.

Instead of landing close to shore, like any cautious and reasonable person might do, I was well out into the lake about 500 metres (545 yards). With the wind picking up from the west, the wave action made it quite choppy, and we were bobbing up and down like a cork. However, ignoring the obvious risk, I proceeded to climb out onto the float and then step up onto the single footrest. This allowed me to get up to where I could reach the fuel cap on the pilot's side wing tank.

I had Larry hand me fuel containers, and I poured in three of them, giving me an extra 54 litres (12 gallons) in that wing tank. While doing this, a specific element of realization finally gripped me when I realized how precarious my situation was, and that inner voice was trying to get my attention.

I was standing on a single footrest, which was only 12 centimetres long by 2.5 centimetres wide (5 inches by 1 inch), with just one foot obviously—my other foot dangled in the air, above the water. The plane was bobbing up and down quite rapidly as the wind was picking up, and wave action was increasing. I realized that I also had no life jacket on, and this water was only around 7 degrees Celsius (45°F), so it would sap a person's energy pretty fast, but then, of course, I couldn't swim so hypothermia wasn't the primary concern.

Are you getting the idea that this was a hazardous situation? A loud inner voice was suddenly screaming, *"What in the world are you doing, look where you are, one slip, and it's all over!"* With that warning fresh in my mind, I climbed back into the pilot's seat and decided I wouldn't put the next two containers in right now, and we took off again.

The further we went north along Highway 37, the worse the weather became. As we approached the Bell 2 Lodge on Highway 37, actually about 25 kilometres (16 miles) south of it, we got hit with a headwind coming slightly from the west that seemed to nearly stop us in midair, and yet the airspeed indicator still showed 110 miles per hour (176 kph).

It took us nearly 18 minutes to make it to Bell 2 when it should have taken around nine minutes. It is located just before a narrow pass where the highway made a *dogleg* to the west. It had 1,689 metre (5,500-feet) elevation peaks on either side, and I was at about 1,220 metres

(4,000 feet) presently. But I was just below the dense cloud layer at around 1,312 metres (4,300 feet) elevation. I couldn't go higher as the cloud-ceiling was down too low. However, as I went through the *dogleg*, you'll see it on Google Earth, the clouds were even lower up ahead, and I was wondering if I could get above them, so I climbed a bit into the clouds to see if there were any openings between them. Nope, nothing, and I knew that I had rock walls on either side of me somewhere in the clouds.

To say I was tense would be an understatement as I started to spiral down to my right as tight as I could through the clouds, to avoid hitting the rock wall. I looked over at Larry, and he was eating peanuts from a bag and offered me some. I just shook my head as my inner thought was, "are you kidding, do you realize how dangerous of a situation we are in right now?"

But I said nothing as my concentration for the moment was on not making a lasting impression on the rock face of these mountains, and becoming a topic of conversation for the oil and gas workers at Bell 2 for the next few months. To say I was asking for *divine intervention* at that moment would be an understatement, but Larry was oblivious to our situation. That was good, I thought, as he wouldn't die all tensed up that way and he'd instantly find himself on the other side and wondering what happened.

On the third spiral down, we finally came out of the cloud, and I was still banking sharply to my right as we broke into a clear sky in front of us and a rock wall not 90 metres (about 100 yards) to my left. If I hadn't kept the spiral as tight as I did, we surely would have done some minor damage to the landscape on that rock face. Coming out below the cloud now, we were only about 275 metres (300 yards) above the highway since the cloud bank that moved in was now much lower. We proceeded north since I had no choice at that point, as there were no landing spots to put a floatplane down in this section of the highway, so we continued.

As we flew north, the clouds got lower and lower, and it was snowing fairly heavily. I wasn't sure where we were as I couldn't recognize any surface features, as visibility was minimal. Then on asking for help, my inner voice pointed out that I could see the tail lights from the semi-trucks on Highway 37 hauling freight up to the Yukon. So, I slowed down to 63 miles per hour (101 kph) just one mile per hour above stall speed and followed tail lights for about 160 kilometres (100 miles) to the Stikine River.

Along the way, we had passed the Bob Quinn Lake Airport and the Tatogga Lake Resort, both of which had bush pilot services operating out of them and a floatplane dock. I never saw either of the lakes, although they were just off the highway since the snow was coming down so hard. All I could do was to focus on the tail lights that were now about 61 metres (200 feet) below me and keep going.

If you're getting the idea that this isn't a recommended method of safe flying, you'd be right. But when you are stuck in a situation where you just can't quit and start over, you have to make do with what you have and ask for *divine intervention*. By the way, if you get yourself into trouble, because you didn't listen to *divine intervention* when the warnings came, and you think that God would not help you now, you'd be wrong. God will never reject you because you've made a serious mistake. Your situation may not be salvageable, and you may now have to live with the consequences, but your guardian angel will walk through it with you and still help in any way possible. You won't most likely be instantly transported to a different situation to escape your consequences, as lessons need to be learned, but you will get help if you ask for it.

We finally started to break out of the blizzard a little as we approached the Stikine River, but due to the stress of the flying conditions and continually looking at the ever-decreasing fuel gauge, I got a bit confused. At that point, I took the wrong direction, flying east along the Stikine for 15 minutes before realizing my mistake and then turning back west and then north once we hit the highway again. By now, one wing tank was empty, and the second one showed that it was down to one-sixteenth of a tank, with the needle just touching on the red line.

We finally had Dease Lake insight, and I could see that there was still a good wind blowing from the southwest. The floatplane base and fueling station was at the very southwest corner of the lake. I was concerned that if I landed anywhere past the dock and the engine quit, we would drift up the 38-kilometre (24-mile) long lake with no way to taxi back if my engine died. I thought I had one chance at this, so I swung out over the lake about 550 metres (600 yards) and then turned back into the wind towards the dock. As I headed into the wind, I hoped I'd make it before my last tank ran dry, which the needle had already told me it was nearly five minutes before.

I came down to about 2.5 metres (8 feet) off the water and kept it there as I headed for the dock. I planned to cut the engine and land close enough to the dock to paddle in. Or perhaps, if the engine died and the plane was still heading in that direction, the momentum would get us close as well.

There was a guy in a small inflatable boat about 36 metres (40 yards) out from the shore, right in front of three guys standing near a truck on the shore watching him and watching this floatplane heading for him. Just as I throttled down to settle down on the water at only about 230 metres (250 yards) from the shore, we caught a gust of wind on the nose that lifted me back up again.

What this gust of wind did was increase the airspeed over the wings, even though we weren't going any faster, but it gave us lift, and we shot up another 4 metres (13 feet). This momentum was a problem since I was doing 63 miles per hour (100 kph). I covered 28 metres (31 yards) a second, and now I was only 183 metres (200 yards) out, and just six and a half seconds from hitting the shore.

This scenario wasn't ideal as I was approaching this panicked individual in the dingy who was pulling on the starter rope of the little outboard as if his life depended on it, and it wouldn't start. The three guys on shore were all standing now and waving their arms frantically to wave me off as if I couldn't see the guy in the dingy. They could see what was going to happen, and possibly they had sentimental feelings for the guy. They didn't possibly realize that a new prop would cost me $10,000, and I wasn't all that interested in hitting the guy anyway. This wasn't in the era when YouTube existed, otherwise they'd have just taken out their cellphones and hoped for a spectacular video to put up online that could go viral like would happen today.

I used the tail rudder and swung slightly to the right, so I wasn't pointed right at the unfortunate guy in the dingy, then hit the throttle in all the way, to cut the engine and dropped my float rudders at the same time. I hit the water just before the guy in the dingy who was probably thinking that he hadn't made out his will yet. I managed to be maybe 6 metres (20 feet) to the right of him, and I then jammed my foot down on the left rudder peddle. I then opened the throttle to give the tail a push from the prop, as I spun around him in a semi-circle so I wouldn't impact the shore just 18 metres (60 feet) in front of me. I was now going 180 degrees in the opposite direction, and not 9 metres (30 feet) from the guy in the dingy, and only about 12 metres (40 feet) off the shore.

I didn't bother to make eye contact with the guy in the dingy as I could feel the heat coming off of him already from where I sat, despite the cool fall temperatures over the water. I suppose he thought I had done that on purpose to scare him, and I would imagine I succeeded. The guys on the shore probably thought I was an idiot, and

I couldn't argue against that, but Larry was chuckling. So, I suspect he thought I was a hot-shot pilot, and just wanted to test out this guy's ability to stay calm on the water, while a large meat chopper was barreling down on him. I bet he threw that little outboard motor away after that.

I was down, but it wasn't over as I needed to get to the floatplane dock, so I taxied over, killed the engine, and nosed into the pier. I got out on the float, and as I tried to step up on the dock, I missed it and fell in with one leg, catching myself on the pier before I went up to my chest in the cold water. My legs were like "jelly" as I was the only person in that plane that realized how close we came to making the news.

I imagine Larry was having a good time as he had a smile on his face throughout it seemed. I got up to check the wing tanks and found that the right tank was bone dry, and the left tank had just over 4.5 litres (1 gallon) in it.

I don't remember the name of the gentleman who owned the floatplane base at Dease Lake in the 90s, but he flew a Beaver out of there the year we got our caribou and now had a twin-engine Otter. He came out to refuel me, and the first thing he said was, "Where in the hell did you come from today?" I told him I came up from Telkwa, and he just shook his head. He said nobody is flying today. All bush pilots have grounded operations due to the bad weather coming up from the south. They've even stranded hunters out all over the region because they won't fly, and you flew through it!

I said we ran into some bad weather and heavy snow, but I followed the tail lights on semi-trucks along the highway to get here. The guy stared at me with an open mouth for a moment, then closed his eyes and shook his head, then murmured something like, *"Ignorance is bliss!"* as he topped me up with fuel, and then we were off again, flying north to Dick Lake.

On arrival at the tiny lake, there were already tents set up on the only decent camping spot. We didn't want to intrude as it was a small lake and knew the outfitter would be upset if we did. So, we flew southwest to Tooya Lake and circled it a couple of times and then put down near the south end as there was a hunting lodge near the north end and a floatplane docked there. But after going ashore, there wasn't a decent place to camp, so we tried to lift off but couldn't get airborne.

Tooya Lake was at 1,121 metres (3,674 feet) in elevation, whereas Tyhee Lake, where we initially took off from, was at only 519 metres (1,700 feet) in elevation. I taxied over to the shore and pumped out the floats, which had taken on a fair bit of water, probably back at Telkwa, and I also dumped out the firewood from the float compartments. Then we could take off, but it still took a very long surface run to build up enough speed and lift. We then flew south to look at an area around Meszah Peak and then east over to the south end of Rainbow Lake about 93 kilometres (58 miles) east from Dease Lake and put down to make camp as the weather was getting bad again.

We didn't shoot anything that trip, which is why this story is in this book and not the other one that involves hunting adventures. But we talked for hours in the tent as Larry was at a turning point in his life. He wasn't happy with his job delivering the Edmonton Journal newspaper from Whitecourt to Foxcreek and Valleyview, Alberta, every day without fail for many years. He was treated badly by every new delivery manager they hired, with continual pay cuts, but he felt stuck. The stress and pressure of how they had treated him over the years was getting to him, affecting his relationship with his family and he needed a change.

I encouraged him to trust in God and quit his job, then start over with something he would enjoy rather than endure this until he died. I believe he left that job not long after and was a happier man for it, especially after the Edmonton

Journal management came to his home, begging for him to continue. After years of abuse and threats and reduced pay on his contract, he refused and sent them packing. That must have felt so good!

So many things on this trip would have ended badly, and yet, I am here to write about this years later. But this is one of those trips that I would never want to repeat, and if it wasn't for a great effort from my guardian angel and *divine intervention,* there is no way we would have made it. Only by *divine intervention*, were we saved from the countless errors I made while preparing for that trip.

Knowing the plane was overloaded and not taking safety measures on the lake when refueling put both of us in peril. Then, there was the insane decision to try and fly through the clouds at Bell 2, forcing me to have to spiral down to avoid looking like a bug on a windshield and then having to follow the tail lights of semi-trucks on the highway through a blizzard. Then making the wrong turn at the Stikine and wasting more fuel, to nearly hitting the guy in the dingy at Dease Lake.

I believe *divine intervention* also played a hand on our arrival at Dick Lake in finding tents already there to prevent us from landing. Since Dick Lake was at a higher altitude than Tooya

Lake and much, much shorter, we never could have lifted off again even after the plane was made lighter.

So many things could have ended in a catastrophe, and yet with God's help, we survived, despite my carelessness. I think the term, *'Ignorance is bliss!'* was an appropriate description for me in this circumstance, and might apply in many cases where God has to bail you out of a bad situation of your own making. But through it all, if I hadn't listened to that guidance and trusted where it was coming from, I never would have made it through. Do you listen? Or do you reject that guidance and take your chances? The morgues and prisons are filled with people every day who choose not to listen.

# CHAPTER TWENTY-SIX

# It Was Too Short

My white-knuckled adventures with my Super Stinson floatplane were not over—it seemed. My eldest son, who was about 14 at the time, and I, were planning a hunting trip for stone sheep to a tiny lake called Little Blue Sheep Lake that was 107 kilometres (67 air miles) northeast of Dease Lake. But before that took place, I wanted some insurance that I could take off at higher altitudes and had a brand-new variable pitch prop ordered and installed on my Super Stinson. Instead of an 82-inch (205 cm), I now had an 88-inch (220 cm) propeller. Yes, in this case, size does matter! That additional 6 inches (15 cm) on the outside of the prop circle spinning through the air, grabbed an awful lot more "real estate" than one might realize. It amounted to a 15 percent increase in air being pulled over the wing surfaces. CF-ABC was indeed an unmatched hot rod on Tyhee Lake and could out-perform any other type of STOL aircraft on takeoff carrying an equal load.

This time, I also had bought collapsible air-craft fuel bladders that hooked right up to the fuel lines in the wing tanks and ran off of a small electric fuel pump that would move the fuel from the bladders to the wing tanks at the flip of a switch. No more standing on 12.5 square centi-metres (5 sq. inches) of a footrest with one foot, to pour fuel into a wing tank! This addition effec-tively nearly doubled my available flight time before I needed to refuel.

But there was another reason for the trip it seemed. A couple of weeks before we departed, I started to hear my inner voice tell me that I had to talk to Justin about a deeper spiritual relationship. Now I fully understand that there are many inter-pretations of what that entails, depending on what denomination you might attend. I'm not here to tell you what you need to believe and that you are wrong if you don't agree with me. I'm just ex-plaining what I felt I was being directed to do by *divine intervention*, based on what I understood a deeper spiritual relationship was, and what I had experienced when I was 21 years old, and still had to that day. And also, what I had witnessed dozens of others experience over the years, after desiring to move into a deeper spiritual experience with God.

Whatever your stance is on the subject, I hope it is the result of personal knowledge derived from fact and not from fiction, which might have been acquired by listening to the opinion of others, who also may not have had any real experience with the subject. However, everyone is welcome to their opinion and to believe in a way that allows them to feel the most comfortable, as we are not all designed the same.

I can only speak for what I have experienced in my life. Like aspects of *divine intervention*, if you have not personally experienced it, then your opinion is solely based on your suppositions, from what you've heard from others and your doubts. I would suggest that; relying on someone else's opinion as your only evidence can be insufficient for many things in life and is not a good substitute for factual evidence and first-hand experience.

I offer this story precisely like all the rest. It is truthful in every way and written as we experienced it. It is real to us, and no one else's opinion, to the contrary, could change those facts.

While organizing the flight plan for this trip, I noted on the aeronautical maps that Little Blue Sheep Lake was at an elevation of 1,374 metres (4,500 feet). The larger Blue Sheep Lake, to the northwest about 9.5 kilometres (6 air miles) away, was at 1,203 metres (3,940 feet) in elevation. It also showed the small lake to be about 800 metres (half a mile) long, so I believed with the new propeller, I would have no problem taking off from there. *Hubris* and a lack of accurate detail, is a dangerous thing if what you are told or have read isn't what reality shows itself to be.

We left one early September morning and flew to the area with our extra fuel tanks on board, without having to stop for fuel at Dease Lake. There was patchy cloud throughout the region, but I managed to locate surface features that matched the map I had, so I knew we were close as we had no GPS (global positioning system) in the plane in the early 90s. I was up at 1,525 metres (5,000 feet) in altitude, so I thought I was above the lake by at least 152 metres (500 feet), and yet all I could see in front of me was a mountain.

It was at that point that I realized that the lake might be much higher up than the map indicated. I continued to climb up as I circled near where the lake was supposed to be, and as I topped the crest of the ridge, there it was.

The Little Blue Sheep Lake was at 1,685 metres (5,518 feet) in altitude, not 1,364 metres (4,500 feet), and that makes a big difference in air density and takeoff. We passed over the lake a couple of times and noticed that there was a lot of exposed rock in it and more just under the surface. There was a tent setup at the very east end of the lake, but no one was around. We suspected it was the outfitter who had left it there all season. We came around and landed into the wind, which was from the southwest and then taxied back to the shallow end.

We then discovered that we couldn't even get close to shore and had to wade in. I found a spot further down the lake on the north shore where we could float the plane over and tie up to the boulders with a couple of long ropes.

After setting up camp, we started to glass the mountains around us for any sign of rams. The only wildlife we encountered, however, were two marmots who became accustomed to stealing food from the tent. They were quite adept at getting in and going through the packs to find what was in easily opened packages.

Later that day, a Super Cub airplane came in and landed, dropping off a hunting guide. It then left and returned with a client from Germany, and left again. The hunting guide was a girl in her 20s, the daughter of the outfitter, and we chatted for a while. She was very accommodating and offered to give us a hand if we needed it. They hunted that day and all the next day, and then the two of them walked away, and we never saw them again.

All the time we were up there, I was continually listening to that inner voice telling me that I needed to talk to Justin, and I was avoiding it. I have always felt that my children needed to make up their minds about God, with a little guidance from me, and didn't want them to feel cornered, but of course, the job of a parent is to provide instruction in life. I thought I could do this back home instead of up here in the mountains, so I wasn't in a hurry.

The church we attended at that time was the Christian and Missionary Alliance Church of Canada, and this one in particular (as I don't know what they all believe) did not believe in a deeper spiritual relationship, in the same way, that I had experienced it. They believed that in time, everyone would figure out what their gift was. But I had never met anyone from there or any church which believed that way, who had exhibited the gifts according to how the Bible described them. But of course, I haven't met all people under that persuasion, so it's just my opinion from what I had experienced myself. Everyone is entitled to believe what they choose to, and what witnesses with their spirit, but I prefer to believe what I have experienced, rather than just what I was taught—there's a significant difference.

With no sign of sheep in the area, I had decided that we needed to have a look around from a better vantage point, from up in the plane, of course, and then go after them the next day. That is legal since it would be well past the required six-hour wait after flying before you could go hunting. We got in the plane, with nothing else but our rifles, as we didn't want to leave them lying around in the tent. After moving out into the lake, I cut the engine and allowed the slight wind to sail the plane in reverse, as far to the east end as possible before our floats touched bottom.

For non-sea plane pilots and non-pilots, in general, you might not have realized that you can sail a floatplane just like a boat by using the flaps, ailerons, and tail rudder just like the sails on a small sailboat. By the time we were as far back as we could get, it didn't look great. Instead of having half a mile to take off, we only had 460 metres (about 500 yards) of water, with a 15-metre (50-foot) sheer rock wall at the west end of it. This obstacle meant we'd have to be off the water in 275 metres (300 yards) to climb out over it. Generally, at an altitude of 460 metres (about 1,500 feet), that would be easy, but we were at 1,685 metres (5,500 feet) altitude now.

There was a very slight headwind of about 8 kilometres per hour (5 mph) coming from the southwest, and I opened the throttle all the way. We were off down the lake, and I lifted off in about 180 metres (200 yards) by jumping the plane out of the water to reduce water drag on the floats. But we were not gaining enough airspeed to climb out with the airspeed indicator sitting right at 63 miles per hour (101 kph), just one mile per hour (1.5 kph) above stall speed. As we approached the rock wall at speed and only 4.5 to 6 metres (15–20 feet) above the surface, I heard a voice screaming that we weren't going to make it over the rock. It was the screaming in my head I was listening to and not the audible screaming that would come just before we hit the rock wall.

I slammed the throttle in all the way, cutting the engine, and we dropped to the water like a rock. There was a large rock outcropping sticking up 4 metres (13 feet) on a small island, just 18 metres (60 feet) out in the lake away from the rock wall. I came down in the water alongside it, and I dropped the float rudders and jammed my foot down on the left rudder peddle, and gunned the engine to spin the airplane around the rock. My 38-foot wingspan (11.6 metres), meant that my wingtips were just 3 metres (10 feet) or so off the rock face and 4.5 metres (15 feet) off the rock outcropping. My left hand on the control yoke was white as I had a death grip on it, and there was little blood flow.

Have you ever had sweat pouring off your brow in 10 degrees Celsius (50°F) weather, and you aren't exerting yourself any more than sitting on a seat in a plane that had no internal heaters?

Then I heard the voice again, *"You are supposed to stay here and talk to your son about a deeper spiritual relationship."* So, my question is, "Would you do what I did next in that situation?" I returned to the starting point and tried again.

This time, we got a little higher, about 9 metres (30 feet) off the water before we had to hit the surface hard and bounced. We then spun around the rock outcropping just as I did before, narrowly missing the rock on either side of my wingtips. Okay, I'm stubborn but not entirely stupid; please hold your comments and laughter. We were spared from certain death twice. I wasn't going to push it a third time. I conceded that I would talk to my son as I was directed, and the inner voice was quiet after that. So, we returned the plane to where we tied up and got out.

That late afternoon, I explained what I had wanted to share with him and revealed my personal experiences from years before. We had a genuine discussion and meaningful time of sharing and relaying my knowledge on the subject.

Regardless of what anyone else chooses to believe, I have never had anyone not experience a deeper spiritual relationship, once it was adequately explained. And that accounted for many dozens of people up to that point in my life without a single failure.

I'm not an evangelist or preacher, it is just something God expected of me from time to time, and I reluctantly consented to the situation.

That evening, the Super Cub returned with supplies for their camp, and I went over to talk to the pilot. I asked him, "How do you fly your clients off this lake?"

He said, "You can't fly anyone off this lake or even lift off with a loaded airplane." Their clients and guides have to walk 11 kilometres (7 miles) down to the larger Blue Sheep Lake, and only an empty Super Cub with half fuel can take off from this lake. Then he left, and we never saw him again. I also noted that the pilot appeared to be a beefy 61 kilograms (135 pounds) compared with my 107 kilograms (235 pounds).

So, this presented a problem. I couldn't have my 14-year-old son walk 11 kilometres (7 miles) down the mountain and up around the valley to try and find their camp at Blue Sheep Lake, with no marked trail and all by himself. He would most likely get lost, not having much bush experience without me around, and if he didn't show up at their camp, I'd certainly panic.

The next day we prayed about it and thought we had a plan. I would make an attempt by myself, carrying just half of our gear and see if I could clear the rock face. We loaded the plane, and Justin held the video camera on shore to catch my final moments when I either went over the rock or tried to go through it.

I backed the plane up as far as I could as usual, and I waited for a little bit of headwind. Once there were small ripples in the water, I opened up the throttle and headed down the lake. I was off again at the same distance, and it slowly climbed but not fast enough. I was right at stall speed still and couldn't gain any more altitude, so I used the rudder to move the plane over slightly to the right, where the slope of the rock face dropped to around 12 metres (40 feet) in elevation.

As I approached it, I tilted the plane over on its right side to raise the left float. I cleared the rock by just 1.5 metres (5 feet) at most, while my son watched me disappear, dropping down over the ridge, as I gained airspeed since the plane had stalled in the air.

I flew to the south end of Cry Lake, a distance of 67 kilometres (42 miles) by air, and coasted up to a sandbar to unload the gear amidst the tracks of a wolf pack that had just passed by that spot. I then returned to Little Blue Sheep Lake and loaded up the other half of the gear and flew it down to the north end of Blue Sheep Lake just 11 kilometres (7 miles) away and unloaded it on their dock. I then returned for the most substantial package, being my son, and landed at the lake one more time. I had, of course, burned off a little fuel by then, so the plane was lighter.

Justin got in, with our rifles, and we said a short prayer. Then I hit the throttle again as we headed into a slight headwind. But just after we had lifted off, the wind died, and we settled back down to the water. This change brought a sense of panic to my chest, but we kept going, and all of a sudden, the plane seemed to *spring* into the air, and we cleared the rock face without having to tilt it over to save the floats from taking a beating.

We landed at both lakes and loaded our gear, and then headed to Dease Lake for fuel as we were low at that point.

Can you recognize *divine intervention* in this story, I certainly did? We should have crashed into the rock face twice while attempting to take off the day before. And I guarantee you that if you told an experienced bush pilot to do that on purpose, he'd tell you that you were nuts. He'd never attempt to drop to the surface and spin a floatplane around a rock island with only 4 metres to spare on either wingtip, but we did it twice.

However, I had a task to fulfill that I was made aware of weeks before. Why I couldn't just talk to Justin back at home while sitting in our truck drinking a Slurpee, I have no idea. I guess maybe it was because; I needed to see how significant God could be in protecting us until I completed this task. It also created a memory that we won't ever forget.

The last take-off was genuinely amazing. As we settled back on the water, halfway through our run, then we sprang up in the air as if being lifted by a hand to guide us over the rock wall with room to spare. I don't wish for anyone to go through experiences I have had to, in order to learn—to trust God. But I suppose if I hadn't experienced these things, then all of these stories wouldn't exist, and if even just one person finds comfort in them enough to trust God in a crisis, it's been worth it.

# CHAPTER TWENTY-SEVEN

# Forced Down

After we left Little Blue Sheep Lake, we flew to Dease Lake and refueled at the floatplane base. My son Justin and I then flew further up north to find a more accommodating lake to hunt from, and after looking at a couple, we headed for the north-shore of Meek Lake. We circled the lake a couple of times and then tied up on shore, two-thirds of the way down the lake near a large rock outcropping on the shore, on that side of the lake. We set up our tent and tried calling moose from there but had no success. We had seen a bull moose at the very northeast end of the lake the day before, which was 5.6 kilometres (3.5 miles) to the east. The next day, we used the plane as a boat and just coasted over there without taking off, but we did not see any trace of it after that first day.

The next day, I had a feeling that we should return home as the real reason for the trip was over. But I decided that I would take Justin up to Dick Lake and let him shoot a caribou, even if there was another camp set up there, as he deserved a chance like anyone else. I knew we could now take off from Dick Lake as it was longer than Little Blue Sheep Lake and at a lower elevation by over 305 metres (1,000 feet). We left the tent at Meek Lake and departed early in the morning, so we would have the required six hours of wait time before we could hunt. That way, we would still have part of the day to look for caribou, but God had other plans.

After circling over Meek Lake to gain altitude, I made a direct run towards Dick Lake at 2,000 metres (about 6,550 feet) altitude. I wanted to clear all the mountain tops in the area, but as we approached Highway 37, just 18 kilometres (11 miles) away, things changed. As we crossed Highway 37 on a straight route between Meek Lake and Dick Lake, oil started streaming up the windshield and not just a trickle. It was a real gusher.

My side of the windshield was quickly covered as I searched the flight map for a body of water to put down along the highway heading south. I found one and headed for it, but it looked too short, so I passed on it and took the next one.

I came down between the trees lining the river that fed the lake from the north and landed in the lake, then taxied to the far shore until my floats touched sand and rocks.

I got out on one float and could see the bottom through the clear water, and with hip waders on, I stepped into the water to tow the plane closer to the shore and tie it up. But that didn't happen. When I stepped on the lake bottom, it disappeared beneath my feet, and I sank as if it wasn't even there. It was super soft silt that had no density to it, and I grabbed the float as I was up to my chest in the lake already, and pulled myself back up onto it. A bit shocked, I forgot about getting to shore to tie up and just opened the cowling right there to see what the leak was. It appeared that I had not latched the lever on the engine dipstick when I checked the oil before taking off that morning, and that was all it was, but we had lost at least two litres of oil. I had one litre with me, and I put it in, and we then decided to head back to camp so I could get some dry clothes on.

Despite the continued feelings that we should return home, I fully intended to take off again and head up to Dick Lake, because I'm stubborn or haven't you realized that yet. As we coasted towards the shore and the little sandy beach where the tent was standing, I got out on the float to step off onto the ground and promptly slid off the float into the lake and got soaked again. Now most rational people would get the message that if I continued in trying to get to Dick Lake, things would continue to get worse— so who's going to blink first. Well, I did!

I told my son that I had a *feeling* we should return home, and he agreed, as he had also had enough excitement over the past few days to last him for a while. So, we packed up our gear, loaded the plane, and headed to Dease Lake for more fuel and then the long flight back to Telkwa, which was 512 kilometres (320 air miles) south from there.

That day, *divine intervention* prevented us from doing what we wanted to do and gave us warnings twice that we weren't supposed to proceed, and it was time to go home. I will never know why we couldn't make it to Dick Lake, but safely arriving back home was all the comfort we needed, and the rest of the trip was uneventful, thank God!

# CHAPTER TWENTY-EIGHT

# Divine Protection

There are hundreds of millions, if not billions of people who have stories to tell, whereby they narrowly missed being injured or killed from events that were not of their own making. We can see them often these days on YouTube, where people miraculously are protected when there are traffic accidents, building collapses, or encounters with wildlife, or other people.

We tend to say that they escaped a tragic accident because they were just lucky. But was it just luck? Is it only the luck of the draw that determines whether this is your day to die? Or is there a larger plan in place that works for your benefit to keep you alive? Unless, of course, you choose to do something incredibly stupid on your own, after many warnings not to proceed, then the results are yours alone to bear.

To my way of thinking, I have experienced many events in my life whereby *divine intervention* was the only explanation for what happened. If you read my second book, *'If Divine Intervention Is Real, Do Hunters Experience It?'* you will see why it's easier for me to recognize it when it occurs, than for someone who has never understood its presence in their lives.

When you suddenly open your mind to recognizing something, you can then see it all around you. Whereas, before your brain was alerted to what you were looking for, you could not see it at all, your mind was cluttered with the concerns of life and never gave it much thought. That doesn't mean it isn't happening, of course, it's just that you don't see it. But if you're a *skeptic*, even if a friend points it out to you, you most likely dismiss it as nothing more than just luck, because you may still wish to defend your skepticism to protect your ego. But then that doesn't mean it isn't happening. It's just that you are willfully blind to it.

I'm sure you can relate to this in some way, and as a simple example, when I was a kid, and we'd go searching for frogs in shallow water, we could hear them croaking all around us but could never see them. You could stand still and focus on the sound right in front of you, but there was no way to recognize the frog until it moved slightly. Then once your brain understood what it was looking for, you could see them all over the place, and they were easy to spot.

The same thing could happen if someone asked you how many red cars you saw in rush hour traffic, in the last hour. If you searched your mind, you might not be able to say for sure that you saw any, or just maybe one or two. From that point on, now alerted to what you are searching for, you can see red cars almost every minute.

It's the same with *divine intervention*. If you aren't looking for it or attuned to it occurring, you can miss it altogether. I'm not talking about obvious situations that are everyday occurrences, like hoping to see a seagull at the beach and voila, there they are, so you claim it was *divine intervention*. No, it wasn't! I'm talking about significant events in your history whereby; it was a *miracle* that it occurred, or you escaped harm, or made it on time, despite the difficulties you faced.

Is there any advantage to walk through life, having the ability to see and yet keeping one's eyes closed in a state of self-induced blindness so that you can say, "It isn't real since I have no evidence that points to it as being the truth because I didn't see it happen?" If one thinks about that approach to life, does it seem logical to you to act that way, simply because you don't want to admit that there is a God, or Guardian Angels, etc. that will work on your behalf to keep you safe until it's your time to leave this world?

Of course, the *skeptic* will always *claim* that science can't prove the existence of God. However, they do not seem to understand the fact that the scientific method can only assess events that repeat themselves or can be intentionally repeated through patterns or actions that can be deliberately measured or tested over and over.

The supra-rational or supernatural is not in the systematic realm of human science, and God is not in the business of having to prove its existence to anyone who has a closed mind or is even unwilling to ask for evidence in their own life.

As I've said previously, not believing in *divine intervention* does not negate the fact that it is real and occurs daily in the lives of hundreds of millions or even billions of people on this planet. It only ensures that the *skeptic* won't experience it, in a way that they will recognize it, because, in the act of preserving pride and ego, they are committed to denying it. Their actions and intent merely deny themselves from realizing the experience; it doesn't deny it from anyone else.

Science creates boundaries and classifies results—whereas the existence of God can only be established individually through intuition, and firsthand experience that verifies God's presence to the individual. This action requires one to open their mind and break down scientific boundaries. Until science is open to researching the mystical path, regardless of the tradition and skepticism of academics, scientists will not even be aware of the limitations of their method and approach. Let alone the ordinary person who relies on the fall back that "science cannot prove there is a God."

We all have an appointed time to leave this world, some earlier and some later, but that does not mean we cannot shorten the timetable by our actions, because after all, we have a free will. If our time is not up, and we find ourselves in a bad situation that is beyond our control and not of our own making, I believe that *divine intervention* is always at hand to keep us alive until our task is complete.

So, along with the many other stories I've told, and the many that will follow as I have two more books to fill, I'd like to share a few instances with you where I recognized *divine intervention* working to keep me alive until my time is up. You will, of course, have many stories of your own. I'm sure if you will allow yourself to recognize them; you can recall them from memory with new insight as to what was at play at the moment. Try it, and you could be amazed at what you find if you purposely search your life for events, where God intervened on your behalf, to allow you to be here now and reading this book, among a million other more important endeavours you will undertake in life.

## Protection from Tragedy, Is A Normal Function Of 'Divine Intervention'

If I had lived a life of relative safety and security, with only a desk job, never risking life and limb, it might be easy to say that I was just not in any dangerous situation, where anything could go wrong. But that's not the case, and along with everything I've told you already, let me give you some examples.

## FORESTRY SCHOOL

One of my first instances where I realized that I had protection from a tragic accident was when I was in the second year of Forestry School in Hinton, Alberta. We were doing a field exercise, traversing through a tall pine forest that had some trees down, from high winds, which we termed "wind-fall" trees scattered along the edge of the cutblock, which is common. I was stepping from one horizontal tree to another when my foot got caught, and I fell forward. I was falling flat out from a standing position as I couldn't move my legs to get them under me. As I came down, I instinctively put my hands out to the next horizontal tree trunk in front of me to break my fall.

Fortunately, I was in good shape back then and could bench press 147 kilograms (325 pounds) and stopped my momentum with my arms. I froze there for a moment and looked down in front of me at the trunk of the tree, where my hands landed. There was a 5-centimetre (2-inch) diameter broken pine branch still attached to the tree, which was about 30 centimetres (12 inches) long. It had been broken off in a spiral, so it formed a dagger point, sticking straight out at me and stopping right at my chest. If I hadn't caught myself in time, or been unable to hold my full weight, my body would have driven onto that spike and drove it through my heart, which is where it was touching me. My mind was prompted at that moment that I had divine protection, as there were things, I was supposed to do in Hinton that were still unfinished. You will find those events, as well as many more acts of divine protection described in my third book, which will be coming in the future.

# FIELD DATA COLLECTION

While working for the Resource Evaluation and Planning Department of the Alberta Government, back in the late 1970s, I had to conduct field data sampling of forest stands all over the province. In one particular area that was very remote, we were flying in a region east of the Steen River Airport, which is north of High Level, Alberta. If you check it out on Google Earth, you can see just how desolate this area is. It was flooded in many areas due to beaver dams at the time and was the only place to put a helicopter down, where there were no trees.

These beaver dams flooded vast areas as the land is quite flat, so you had to walk up to a couple of hundred metres (or yards) in water to get to dry land. But I was already wet anyway because the only way to gain access to the forest cover to gather the field data was to have the helicopter pilot hover about half a metre (or a couple of feet) over the water of the beaver dam. Each person would step out onto the landing skid, and then as the pilot nodded to them, they would jump off into the water.

If a person jumped off before the pilot was ready to compensate for the sudden shift in the balance of the machine, it induced a violent roll to the craft. This weight difference created some very anxious moments on occasion when someone wasn't paying attention to the pilot's instructions. The pilot indicated his readiness with just a head-bob.

The forest stands in this region are very short due to their slow-growing conditions, hardly ever reaching more than 9 to 15 metres (33–50 feet) in height for the deciduous trees. The areas upstream and adjacent to the beaver dam were somewhat clear of trees as the beavers would cut down the aspen and poplar to use as building materials, and food to store for winter. But there were always a few standing dead trees that the beavers ignored and clipping the tops with the 11-metre wide (36 feet) rotor blades was not uncommon if the machine swung too far in one direction or the other.

As you can imagine, the mosquito numbers were extreme in areas of Northern Canada that were flooded like that, as it provided ample stagnant water for them to lay their eggs and multiply. Any creature unfortunate enough to be found in their territory got subjected to a massive swarm of mosquitoes that was so dense that at times at a distance of just 1.5 metres (5 feet), you could not identify the face of the person working with you. All exposed skin and even thin clothing were, of course, soaked in DEET mosquito repellant spray, in an attempt to ward them off long enough to conduct our field data collection. But it seemed at times the bug spray was just the garnish on the main meal when the swarms got too intense.

Ever hear the high-pitched sound of 5,000 mosquitoes buzzing around your face just a couple of centimetres (1 inch) away and flying into your mouth, nose, and even into your eyes? It becomes unbearable, and I can understand how people were driven crazy in the bush by mosquitoes before repellants were available.

The field plots entailed drilling an increment borer into the center of a tree at 1.3 metres (4.3 feet) height and retrieving a core that was 4 millimetres (5/32 inch) in diameter, to count the tree rings, and determine the age of the forest stand. We also measured tree-heights with a Suunto clinometer and recorded the diameters of the trees in the plots.

Try counting 60 years of tree rings on a 4-millimetre diameter core (5/32 inch) that is only 7 centimetres long (2.75 inches) with thousands of mosquitoes in the way. But we worked as fast as possible so that we could retreat to the safety of the helicopter and escape the onslaught of the tiny blood-sucking vampires. If one were unfortunate enough to be stranded in an area such as this, it would be a struggle to survive even one night.

Having the helicopter hover so close to the water surface and to the surrounding trees that remained in the beaver dam, would mean that a rotor strike on either one would result in lots of crumpling metal, screaming, a potential fireball, and tons of regret.

Then, of course, once we had all exited the machine, it lifted off and flew away. Sometimes to only circle the area and other times to fly some distance away and land until we completed our work and the pilot would return at a prescribed time. You would never be allowed to do this today, due to workplace safety regulations, but back in the 1970s, field staff was more expendable, I suspect, or we were just more daring, and so were the pilots. A lot of them had been helicopter pilots fresh out of the Vietnam War and accustomed to operating in conditions where life was expendable.

Then once we finished collecting our plot data, we would have to wade back out into the beaver dam and stand there waiting for the helicopter to return. The reason we had to do this was that, if the pilot did not see us standing in the open spot, he would not try to land when he returned. We didn't have portable radio communications with the pilot back in 1978, so getting out of there depended upon trust. Trust that the pilot would return at the appointed time, and we'd be standing there, in chest-deep water, waiting for him. As autumn began to set in often this required standing in water that had thin ice along the edges where it was shallower and very, very cold.

## PAY ATTENTION

On one occasion, during the Chilcotin contract in 1990, we were asked to use a helicopter that the Williams Lake Forest District had chartered for fire action to cut down on some of the costs. The pilot only had a little over 500 hours, which is the minimum required to fly a commercial helicopter. I wasn't all that pleased with having to use a machine with a pilot with so little flying experience as we had to get into some tiny landing spots to conduct our field data collection. Jim P. and his son were in the back of the machine, and the three of us were doing the field data collection. I was doing the air calls from the front left seat of the machine and navigating for the pilot.

Ironically that morning before we lifted off, Jim had taken his stainless-steel Ruger Blackhawk .44 Magnum out of his shoulder holster to check it near the machine, and this inexperienced pilot had a panic attack. He was terrified of guns and insisted that Jim not carry his firearm. Jim produced the permit from the RCMP, authorizing him to carry the handgun for protection from predatory wildlife while conducting fieldwork in remote areas of B.C.

The pilot then had no choice but to allow it but insisted that it be unloaded in the helicopter as if it would suddenly go off by itself. Therefore, each time Jim exited the helicopter, he had to handle his firearm and load it. Then he had to handle it again and unload it beside the machine before getting back into the helicopter, multiplying the potential for an accident.

The pilot felt much safer with me in the front, although I had a Ruger Redhawk .44 Magnum, in a shoulder holster under my cruiser's vest, fully loaded, all the time during the fieldwork process.

However, the danger to the pilot wasn't from a loaded firearm, as there is no account in history where a loaded firearm suddenly jumped up and started shooting people. This pilot, though, turned out to be far more dangerous than the two .44 Magnums on board.

On the first risky occasion with this pilot, I had picked a rock outcropping on the side of a ridge to get put down on; and had asked him to rest one skid on the outcropping so we could exit the machine, and he could pick us up later the same way. This method is standard practice for helicopter pilots in mountainous terrain where the landing spot is on a slope. But he said, "I think there's enough room to put the whole machine down."

I turned to him and said, "Are you sure it looks way too small?" Okay, he was the pilot in command, with 500 hours. But I had well over 3,000 helicopter hours doing this work and had seen this scenario many times, and was pretty sure he didn't have enough room.

He began to nose the machine forward onto the rock outcropping towards the tall pines in front of us on the slope. We had the front half of both skids on the rock, and I had that inner voice shouting at me again. *"Look what he's doing,"* it said. I glanced at the pilot and saw he was staring down at his skids to see if he could get them onto the flat part of the rock. Then the voice said, *"Look at the rotor blades."* As I quickly glanced up, I could see the tip of the blades spinning dangerously close to the trunk of a tall lodgepole pine.

The 50-centimetre (20-inch) diameter pine in front of us had a small branch no more than about 25 centimetres (10 inches) long sticking out at about the height of the rotor blades. It suddenly disappeared off of the face of the pine, and I felt my eyelids peel back. I quickly glanced at the pilot again, and he still wasn't looking up at his blades. I shouted into the mic, *"back off now."* He jerked the stick backward, pulling us away, and then I pointed out that he just cut a 25-centimetre (10-inch) branch off of that pine.

As we looked for a different plot location, I realized that this pilot isn't aware of his surroundings, and that makes for a very dangerous helicopter pilot. We'd have been a crumpled mass of aluminum and burning flesh as we rolled down the ridge if I hadn't *shouted* at him, and a wave of anxiety washed over me as the adrenalin rush took hold.

Later that day, I had picked a plot location on the edge of a large meadow surrounded by tall spruce trees. The meadow was at least 10 hectares (24.7 acres) in size and flat with half a metre (roughly two feet) tall grass covering it. The plots were just off one corner of the meadow, and I expected the pilot to put the machine down, where I marked the spot with a red "X" on the aerial photo, which was easily 60 metres (65 yards) from the treeline.

But as he came down to treetop level, he kept moving forward up into a tight corner, closer and closer to the trees, and that inner voice said, *"watch out."* I glanced at the pilot, and sure enough, he was staring at his skids again and not watching the rotor blades. I shouted, *"look at your blades"* just before he hit the top of a spruce tree on the right, cutting about one metre (or a little over a yard) length off of it. He then swung us to the left, where he cut the top off another spruce tree. The helicopter was shaking violently; as we backed off 10 metres (11 yards), and he landed. All I could do was shake my head, and we got out to complete the ground plot and collect the field data.

He never said anything to us as we got back in the machine, and as we lifted off, the whole machine was vibrating. I said, *"We're done, take us back,"* even though it was the middle of the day. I wasn't going to take any more chances with this guy, and he proved to me that his concern about our handguns was the least of his problems. I never flew with him again and told the Ministry of Forests what he had done that day and that I wouldn't use their charter machine anymore if he were the pilot.

The first time we were no more than a few inches and two to three seconds from a catastrophic accident on the rock outcropping, and then in a wide-open meadow, he nearly killed us again. Sometimes *divine intervention* has to work overtime to compensate for human error and keep us above ground.

# A SIGNIFICANT ERROR

On another occasion, we were working on a contract located south of Stewart, B.C., and east of the long Portland Canal and included a lot of rugged mountain terrain. We were fortunate enough to have a tiny female pilot, which is a benefit when we had four guys in the helicopter as passengers. The fieldwork was going well, and we were dropped off as two crews, sometimes together and other times separately, conducting field data collection. I had portable aircraft radios by then so that each team could keep in contact with the helicopter as it moved us from plot to plot.

Then a series of careless mistakes placed us in a situation that nearly took our lives. We had just refueled and had headed out to conduct more sampling in a valley as we worked our way up a ridge. The first two landing locations were not suitable to put the machine down into, as there were too many uneven rocks on the ground to keep the machine level. So, we continued to the next location with similar results. We had planned to drop one team off near the top of the alpine area. Then just Justin and I would stay in the machine and continue up into the alpine and land at very high altitude to conduct some plots in short alpine fir.

What we hadn't considered was that we still had almost full fuel, and now four passengers instead of two, and we were up at very high altitude where the trees were only 2–3 metres (7–10 feet) tall. The surface was covered in deep snow up there, but the day was relatively warm, reducing the lift capacity of the helicopter. As we came down to land, the scene looked beautiful with the white snowpack, but I suddenly had a very anxious feeling inside. My inner voice told me to look at the instrument panel, and I could see that we were suddenly pulling 105 percent power on the engine and coming down fast. The problem was that the short stubby and very tough alpine fir trees with very short branches showed no wind direction, and we were coming down with a tailwind, and way overloaded for that altitude. I said, *"Power"* into the mic, and quickly pointed at the gauges. Instantly the pilot put the nose down and skimmed the surface of the snow. We left skid marks along the top of the snowpack as she gained airspeed and pulled nearly 120-percent power to stay in the air, and started to swing around into the wind.

If you are unfamiliar with helicopters, what I know is that if you pull over 105 percent power from the engine, you are required to have a complete inspection done to certify it was airworthy. I don't know what the requirements are after pulling 115 percent for more than 20 seconds, but I suspect something very significant.

## Saved from Disaster

As I think back, there were many other incidents where I knew that *divine intervention* was needed to save the day.

**(a)** When sitting in the passenger seat of my Isuzu Trooper 4x4, an employee wanted to drive, then froze as she slowly drove off the road and up a steep bank on the left and rolled the vehicle over, landing on my side. Fortunately, seconds before this happened, I had a feeling that I should bring my arm back into the car as I had it hanging outside the open window, and it would have been pinned under the truck and destroyed.

**(b)** I was stalked by black bears in remote areas of the coastal mountains that were intent on taking down one of us for a taste, and I had to use my handgun to ensure our safety.

**(c)** I have also crashed a Gyro on floats into a lake and survived. Yes, I bought another RAF 2000 kit and built it, then did my training once I moved from B.C. back to Alberta, and was the first person ever to put that machine on floats, but it never flew again.

**(d)** I also got my hand caught in the drive chain of a rock picker that had the hydraulics still engaged, and as it pulled my hand into the cogs and I strained against it with all my strength, the thought came to me that it was going to tear my fingers off. A voice in my head said, *"Rip your hand out of the leather glove right now, no matter what was torn,"* and I did. Only a second later, the glove was pulled through the cogs and shredded. The adrenalin rush nearly collapsed me, and after that I thought I was having a heart attack. Having time to realize that I would lose all the fingers on my right hand, in the last instant, was like throwing a bucket of ice water down your back on a hot day.

## Consider These Questions

So, convey to me this, what is your opinion as to why I escaped these situations without severe injuries? Or most likely would have even died, if I hadn't been warned? Is God protecting me, more than he does for another person who isn't a believer? Is God showing me favouritism because I acknowledge the presence of a loving supernatural being, and have read scriptures and prayed? Does this kind of thinking allow you to condemn God for being unfair when your friend, or loved one, or even yourself, gets harmed in an accident?

To a *skeptic*, this is usually one of their arguments for not believing in God, and in actuality, they are just *angry* at an entity that they don't even think exists. That's certainly a waste of time, and emotion, wouldn't you think?

Do you think that I escaped all these situations just because God favours me, and because I am somehow more righteous and more deserving? If you do, then you would be DEAD WRONG! God loves everyone equally! In my opinion, the difference in the outcome of tragic events is due to anyone's willingness to LISTEN to what I have come to understand is *divine intervention* working on my behalf. To recognize and respond to the direction of that inner voice, at least most of the time, has spared me from fateful events that I would not be happy to experience? In my opinion and experience, that is—can I ask you ... "Do You Listen?"

I have not listened on many occasions, and experienced something I didn't like; then I was reminded by that same inner voice that I had been warned ahead of time but did not listen. If I had listened, I could have avoided all that mess and later regret, and this has convinced me of its validity. God, or possibly my guardian angel, is great at the *"I told you so,"* aspect of our relationship. And that is as it should be. For if it did not remind me that I was forewarned of an impending horrible outcome after I experienced it, I would never learn to trust it and be willing to listen to it the next time and be spared something possibly far worse!

And anyone who says, "Well, it was just your intuition and visual clues that you picked up on which warned you," is being naïve, and has far more faith in pure luck than it takes to believe in a loving God. And if that were the case, then why isn't that *skeptic* a billionaire already if they believe in luck so adamantly?

Although some instances offered visual clues beforehand, something brought my attention to it, long before it was needed, and you'll read about that in the story entitled: "It's Fresh" in the book containing my hunting activities. But many other situations provided no forewarning or visual clues as to what was coming, and it was only in the instant it occurred, that I had a choice to listen and react, or ignore it and suffer the consequences.

Think about it! How many times have things gone wrong for you, and it made you angry at God, even if you don't believe God exists?

And yet on every single one of those occasions, if you're honest with yourself, you can recall that you had negative feelings and misgivings about proceeding with what you were doing. You had forewarnings that this wasn't a good idea, and it could go wrong, but you dismissed them. Where were those warnings coming from, for you? You went ahead anyway. Now you have to live with the results of being unwilling to listen to *divine intervention*, which was provided by your guardian angel to try and correct your actions before it was too late.

So, for all those people who think they are feeling *justified* at being angry with God for the situation they're in, I can tell you that you only have yourself to blame. There will always be a way of escape provided and early warnings to change your direction, but if you ignore them, and refuse to listen, then the rest is on you. We receive ample *guidance*, but when we disregard it because of our ego telling us that we deserve the outcome, we anticipate, and then our worst fears are often realized.

If you are willing to listen to that inner voice that tries to warn you of impending danger and act upon it quickly, without questioning it or trying to rationalize those thoughts away, then you can experience less pain and struggle in life.

You can keep drawing a breath until it is your appointed time to let go of this life and move on.

We are all going to die someday, but I'd like to finish up whatever I'm supposed to do before that happens and live in a manner of my choosing. So, for me, being willing to listen to that inner voice providing *divine intervention* has been an absolute must to make it this far. And yet, I have failed to listen many times and suffered the consequences and live with the regrets. My goal is to pay attention more often and have fewer difficulties.

I have other instances that were similar to the ones I've listed, but suffice it to say, these give you an idea of how, when, and why your guardian angel might try to intervene in your life to spare you from a tragic outcome. I wouldn't want to go through life too proud and too stubborn to listen to the warnings that are a deliberate means to spare me from grief.

How about you, are those worth it to you, to listen?

# CHAPTER TWENTY-NINE

# Didn't Want to Move

In the summer of 1995, I was having thoughts that perhaps we should move back to Alberta so that our children could be closer to their grandparents. Of course, I realized that ideas like this weren't generally coming from me alone, but being put there by God, because I had no other personal reason to move. We decided to take a summer holiday, the first one ever, and drove to Millet, a small community south of Edmonton, and rented a small motorhome for a couple of weeks.

My first incident of not listening to God was when we picked up the motor home, and my attention was instantly drawn to the rear tires on the vehicle as they looked quite worn out. I asked the manager if those tires are okay, and he assured me they were satisfactory. I should have listened to that inner voice, but I didn't.

We drove from Millet to Drumheller, Alberta, to see the dinosaur museum and had our first flat tire. Of course, it was the inner tire of the dual wheels, so I had to take both of them off to put the spare on, which was almost flat itself. It was on a Sunday, so there were no tire shops open, so I pulled onto an empty lot and got out the tiny jack then proceeded to lift the vehicle.

It was so hot that day that the asphalt was soft where we stopped, and the base of the jack sank into the surface a couple of inches and didn't lift anything. I had to search around the property and found a short piece of lumber to put under it to disperse the weight a bit more and finally got the tire changed. The constant reminder in that heat was that I should have listened to the warning. The tire was destroyed as the sidewall delaminated, so any repair was out of the question. The next day we had to buy another tire before leaving Drumheller. We then drove across Saskatchewan to my hometown of Swan River, Manitoba, and had the second flat tire that shredded itself on the highway, again it was the inner of the dual wheels on the opposite side, and I had to buy another tire.

It was the first holiday we had taken since 1978, and I was spending a good part of it being frustrated. I chose not to listen to the guidance and warning I was given before we left Millet, and changing tires on the side of the road in blistering heat that summer was my reward. After visiting my Uncle Gord, who was a long-haul trucker all of his adult life, he said he wouldn't allow me to leave on those last two tires because they were going to blow at any time, and he was right. After the third flat, I replaced the fourth tire as well. If I had only listened to the warning given to me at the beginning, I could have avoided all of this. But even with my background, I can still be stubborn because after all, I can handle anything, right! Are you that stubborn as well?

Throughout the trip, though, I still had the feeling that we're supposed to move back to Alberta and shared that with my family, who were receptive for several reasons. But I didn't want to move. All of my work projects were in B.C., and yet it was nagging at me that we should move.

I thought that if we didn't find a place we would like on this trip, then we would stay where we were. We had already been looking for more significant properties to buy, out in the country east of Telkwa, with more land than just a yard on the edge of a field. After visiting friends and relatives in Manitoba and with that in mind, we drove back across Saskatchewan and into Bonnyville, Alberta, and had a look at the town. I had driven through there a few times in the past on my way to gather field data plot information back in the 80s and also once when I took a couple of friends from B.C. to Saskatchewan to hunt whitetail deer, and the place seemed interesting.

I was thinking that I would get this over with and put the idea of moving behind us for good, so I walked into a real estate office on Main Street to see what was available. I believed that I would fulfill my part of this urging by the spirit by being told that there is nothing right now that fits my requirements, and we could then return to B.C., and search for places out there.

The real estate agent asked what I would like to see. I said, "I'd like at least 80 acres that were fairly secluded with a decent building site, so we could have a house built. It should be within 20 minutes of town, and if possible, it would also have a lakeshore joining the property, and no more than $80,000." I was reasonably certain I would be off the hook any minute, and we could start planning to stay in B.C.

He sat back in his chair and thought for a moment and said, *"That's pretty specific."*

I nodded and said, "Yep, and I understand if there isn't anything available right now."

He nodded and said, "I think I have something that exactly fits your description."

I was shocked, and just nodded! He asked if I wanted to look at it, and I agreed, so he gave me the sales flyer that had a map on it. I mentioned that we had a few other things to do first, so we'd like to have a look at it ourselves when we could.

I took the flyer with the details about the property down to the motorhome to show my family, shaking my head the whole way. We drove out to the property, which was 18 minutes from town. It was 32 hectares (80 acres) in size and included a privately owned half-mile of sandy beach on the south shore of Muriel Lake south of Bonnyville. It was treed with aspen, poplar, birch, and some spruce except for a 4- to 6-hectare (10-15 acre) patch of grassy field along the access trail into the property. It was just north of the gravel road that skirted the south edge of the lake and was surrounded by crown land, with the nearest neighbours being seasonal lake cabins 5.6 kilometres (3.5 miles) to the west.

It had been a homesteaded property from about 60 to 70 years previously and had never had a house built on it. It was a combination of excitement that this was the perfect spot and disappointment as I didn't want to move back to Alberta. The family seemed to like the place though and especially the beach, although the water was some distance out, as the lake was lower now than a decade earlier apparently.

My only way out of this deal was the price, which was listed at $200,000. We decided that we would make an offer on the property anyway, as it had been exactly what I had requested. I was sure an offer of $80,000 wouldn't buy the place, so I was going to stick to it. It turns out that the original owner of the property had died decades earlier and had left it to two relatives in his will, and it had been for sale for quite a while, and neither of them lived locally.

When I went back to the real estate agency, I said I would make an offer, and of course, he was happy, but I was not! However, I did, and he was a little shocked at my proposal. I told him that I understood if they couldn't let it go for $80,000, it was a beautiful piece of property and I'm sure they will get an offer closer to what they're asking.

We returned the motorhome to Millet and picked up our truck and drove to Barrhead, Alberta, where my wife's parents lived, to visit with them. I think she told them we had made an offer on some property near Bonnyville, but I can't remember for sure. I got a telephone call from the real estate agent while we were there, as we gave him the house number before we left. He said that the landowners had a counteroffer of

$180,000. I said thanks, but I won't make a counteroffer and appreciated his time. The next day he called back and said that they had another counteroffer of $120,000, to which I gave the same response and said that I would be travelling to Whitecourt the next day and then back to B.C.

He asked if there was another number, he could have for there, and I reluctantly gave him the telephone number of a friend's place where we would be staying. But now I was getting nervous.

You see, because I didn't want to move, I had put up a *fleece*, which said "that all the things I wanted had to be on the property, and in addition to that, it had to be for $80,000." If God wanted us to move, then that fleece had to be fulfilled, and why should I make it easy? After all, he's God, right!

We travelled from Barrhead to Whitecourt, our old stomping grounds and visited with old friends for a day or two, and a few other friends in the area. While there, the telephone rang, and it was the real estate agent again. I was reluctant to take the call but did out of courtesy, and he said, *"They accepted your offer of $80,000."* My heart sank, and I said thanks and hung up. I don't suppose you have ever heard of such a reluctant buyer of a piece of lakefront property that came down from $200K to $80K and was sad about it, have you? I bet my guardian angel was chuckling, though.

How could it be a coincidence that every detail I requested for the property in the fleece, was spot-on with the first and only inquiry we made at a real estate office on the entire trip? And then that the price of $80,000 also met, if *divine intervention* was not responsible for what took place? At this point, for any rationally thinking person, it should take a lot more faith to believe that it was all just a coincidence than to accept the fact that God orchestrated this whole thing. But the various confirmations that we were doing the right thing weren't over yet, as I needed more assurances.

# CHAPTER THIRTY

# The Little Bush

After paying for the property and now that it was ours, I ordered the aerial photography so that I could look it over in detail and decide where I would have the house and the shop built. As I drew out the boundaries of the buildings, I was wondering where we would drill a well. And one night while half asleep, or half awake and dreaming, I could vividly see the surface of the property in my mind from the aerial photography as I stared up at the ceiling in our bedroom.

As I asked the question, "where do we put the well?" I noticed a tiny *bush* located between where the house would be and the north corner of where the shop would be. For some reason, that little bush seemed to stand out, and it was small, only a little over a metre high and wide (roughly 4 feet high x 3 feet across). It was slightly separated from the rest of the bush on the west side of the clearing by about 3 metres (10 feet). I had the most definite feeling that I was supposed to have them drill there.

By the second weekend in October, we were back in Alberta for the long weekend and revisiting the property on the Saturday before Thanksgiving Day. I knew that *dowsing* worked as I had seen it happen before. Very gifted people can tell you exactly how deep to drill as well. Forget the name well-witching, as it has negative connotations around it that are based on the superstition that some people just aren't able to let go of. They allow their irrational fears and imaginations to overtake their rational thinking and begin to fear the simplest things.

I believe water well dowsing stems from something within the electrical field of the individual, which is attracted to the movement of water underground. It has NOTHING to do with being a witch any more than what a chiropractor does! It is used all over the world to locate underground pipes, watercourses, and of course, where to drill for water wells. Just because you can't explain something, you shouldn't be afraid of it, and then tell everyone else to be scared of it also. That's how innocent people got burned at the stake in history, based on the fearmongering of misinformed zealots. But once again, a *skeptic* is just someone who doesn't have practical experience with a subject, and it does not mean their opinion is correct, but it does mean their opinion can be dangerous.

I can't rationally explain why so many incredible events happened in my life that were well beyond fate or pure luck, and I can only see the EVIDENCE of *divine intervention*, not the entity or power behind it. It is the eyewitness evidence that I believe, and I try not to let my irrational fears control my rational or logical thought process, as I tend to be quite analytical.

I read up on dowsing, and it said that roughly one in five people could do it, and there were five of us, so what do you think the chances are that it might be one of us?

We went out to the property on Saturday morning, and I cut some "Y" shaped willows for us to try some dowsing before the well driller arrived. We split up, and each walked all over the property near where the house would be built. I certainly wasn't feeling anything, and neither did anyone else. When I walked out of the trees, from the west side of the clearing, I happened to be standing near that little bush that I saw in my mind, as I had looked up at the ceiling in my bedroom in B.C., months before. I could hear the drilling trucks coming into the property, so I shrugged and took out some orange seismic ribbon and tied it around the bush, just as the well drilling truck pulled up.

The well driller came up to me as I stood near the little bush and asked me where I wanted him to start drilling, and I pointed to the ribbon. He asked if we dowsed it, and I said "no." He then told me that he had drilled for water all over the south end of the lake and had gone down to over 120 metres (400 feet) on many occasions with no success. He said there was a shale layer, and once you hit that, there is nothing below it. Since we were at a lower elevation than the cabins further west on the lake, we'd probably hit the shale in a short distance, and drilling below it is just a waste of money, as he's done it many times in this area. Of course, I have to pay the same amount of money for a dry hole as one that hits water.

I asked him where all the people living along the lake get their water from, and he said that they have long water lines out into the lake and pump lake water to their homes. Well, that wasn't going to work for me as the water was easily 137 metres (150 yards) out, and then it was so shallow you could walk another 91 metres (100 yards) before you got your knees wet. That might be fine in summer, but for year-round living, it wouldn't work in winter, when the ice froze to the bottom far beyond that point. With that *warning* out of the way, he started drilling, and we continued look around the property.

After a couple of hours, he called me over to him and showed me the cuttings that were coming up from the drilling and said we are into the shale now, and it was only 12 metres (40 feet) down. He said there wouldn't be any water below this as he's tried dozens of times. I turned away from him and looked out at the lake and talked to God. I said in my mind, "What do I do now, Lord; this was the only spot you told me to mark?"

I then looked back at him and didn't say anything. I suspect he could see the dejected expression on my face, and said, "We'll drill one more stem and see how deep the shale is, just to see what happens." I nodded, and I stood there as they connected another 6-metre (20-foot) length of pipe and started the drill stem rotating. It had taken over an hour to drill 12 metres (40 feet), and within about five minutes, the drill stem started moving down rapidly into very fine, wet gravel. The whole 6 metres (20 feet) then disappeared in just a couple of minutes more, and he turned to me with wide eyes after picking up a handful of the cuttings. *"You'll get water now,"* he said, and then they added one more stem, and it too drilled down in just over three minutes.

He shut off the drilling unit and left the drill stem in the hole to keep it open. Then said they would come back tomorrow and finish the well, as he hadn't brought any well-casing with him since he never expected to find any water. Some more chuckling in the spirit world by the guardian angel, I suspect.

I was elated, of course, but I wondered how good the well would be, as in how many litres or gallons per minute it would produce in drawdown recovery. You need at least 27 litres (6 gallons) per minute to have a workable well out in the country, being your only water source.

I told him we were going to have a look at the Alliance Church in Bonnyville for Thanksgiving Sunday and then come out after, and he said that's fine, as he'd already be there in the morning.

The next day we went to the Alliance Church on the west side of town to see what they would be like, as we had tried the Pentecostal Church in July when we first went through town. To our dismay, not a single person spoke to us as strangers, even though we walked up as a family and sat right near the front and stayed for the whole service, and then walked past everyone as we then left the church. Everybody was too busy chatting with their friends and didn't want to bother themselves with strangers. It's a sad state to get into for many churches, and not even the pastor made an effort to greet us. They were all dressed to the nines in their best attire and had come there to impress each other, not to display the image of God and Jesus to strangers who were dressed like holiday tourists—so sad I thought as we walked out the door and down the front steps and never went back.

It was a different experience at the Alliance Church; everyone wanted to talk to us and find out more about us, including the children talking to our kids. So, we knew where we might be coming when we returned the next summer after we had our house built. While we mingled after the service, the church secretary walked up to the pastor and said something, then looked at us, and he then came over to where we were standing.

He said that there was a telephone call for us and I could take it in his office, which I did. It was weird as the only person who knew we would be there was the well driller, and of course, that's who it was. He said that we needed to come to the property right now to look at the well. I asked if there were problems as you said we would get water. He said, "yes, you have water, but you'd better have a look."

So being a little worried, we drove out to talk to him, still dressed in our Sunday best, as they say. He said, *"Watch this,"* and they started their compressor pump, which was blowing air down the well to determine the amount of recovery in gallons per minute it can produce. The water was coming out of a side port on the main stem and filling a 225-litre (50-gallon) open-top tank.

He pumped for 20 minutes with the tank overflowing the whole time. Then shut off the pump and lifted the 6-metre (20-foot) stem that was inside the casing and said, *"Look here."* The water was 15 centimetres (6 inches) below the surface after all that pumping. He said, "Your recovery can't be measured, but it is at least 200 gallons per minute." He then smiled at me and said, "How did you do this, you dowsed it, didn't you?"

I said, "No, I just thought God told me to drill here." He didn't know what to say except that this was the only place out of 40-plus homes along the south shore that will have its own well.

We also had to get a road built into the site as all that currently existed was a grass trail. I prayed about that and noticed some grassed over mounds on the east side of the access trail, about 182 metres (200 yards) away. On examining them, I discovered that it was pure small grit gravel without any clay or dirt in it, and there were thousands of cubic metres, (or cubic yards) of it. I contacted a road construction contractor to come out and have a look, and he built us a beautiful road in just half a day with materials from right on the property. What more could one ask, right, as it only cost me an hourly charge for the road grader, plus a gravel truck and backhoe to load the truck for a few hours?

So, for my skeptical readers, tell me how it could be just a coincidence that I saw that small bush in my mind while slipping off to sleep, 1,600 kilometres (1,000 miles) to the west of there, and months before, and could also find it on the aerial photos? Then once at the property again, felt it was the right place to drill—and hit an artesian well that the experienced well driller in this area would have sworn was impossible on the south shore of this lake? To the believers, realize that as easily as God found water for us in this challenging situation, he can find you the job you want, the person you are supposed to be with, or the place you are supposed to move to. Your only responsibility is to trust, and he'll do the rest. Ask him now and use my experience as an example. I'm sure God won't mind! Then be patient and watch what happens.

# CHAPTER THIRTY-ONE

# It's Not Been Perfect

It may seem as if God intervening in my life on so many occasions demonstrated in both small and large miracles that life has been a piece of cake for me. That any time I doubted, God always came through and saved the day, and your experience just hasn't been as fortunate as mine. You may even think that I don't know what it is like to fail because I've always had a safety net. The truth, unfortunately, is far from that!

As a person who has tried to meet the needs of everyone around him, I have discovered that it takes a toll on you emotionally, spiritually, and physically. Being a person who could feel the pain of others is the result of an excess of empathy, and some people might call that person an empath. The problem with sensing the suffering of others, listening to their troubles, and taking on their struggle to try and help them, is that you have no control over their actions; however, you may think you do.

I can't count how many times I've had people come to me with problems and ask for advice. It's called *dumping* on someone else, by the way. Now, I'm not opposed to that—as where else are you going to find good advice if you don't ask someone you trust. The problem lies in the fact that most of the time, they don't take the advice, even though the solution is easy to see from the outside. It's because they are so committed on a personal level, and their ego is so involved, that they can't accept that good advice, and end up going their way, anyway.

It often ends in disaster, and it tore my heart apart to watch their suffering because it wasn't necessary and could have been avoided, had they listened when they had a chance. Okay, I fully understand how it affects me; and it is not their fault. Being overly sensitive and trying to fix everything for everyone is my problem to deal with in my life. But it can take its toll on the nervous system of an empathic person, and it isn't visible on the outside until it's too late.

Because we moved several times for work, I attended eight different churches in four different denominations. In the smaller towns, they'd ask for me to be on the board as a deacon or elder. After the first time, I agreed to do this, I always refused to act in this capacity because of all the politics, backbiting, and kowtowing to look good, that I saw taking place. But I would eventually give in and took on the responsibilities in a new setting, hoping it would be better. The problem was; I was even closer to feeling the pain, anger, and frustration, and witnessing the indiscretions of those in leadership.

Because I was deemed to be fair and impartial, I would become the person everyone came to for help, especially if they had problems with the pastor or other members of the congregation. At one point in my last position as an elder, I was receiving up to 14 phone calls a day from people who had grievances and needed someone to listen and help them find a solution. This amount of time may not seem like much to someone with those responsibilities in a large church, but I was also working 12 hours a day on my forest inventory contracts.

You might think it's lovely that people would confide in me and seek guidance. But you wouldn't if you were someone who felt everyone's emotional state, gave thoughtful advice to help solve the dilemma, and then watched them ignore it, and see things go from bad to worse. That frustration takes its toll, and there are millions of people in and out of churches who know, precisely, what I am talking about, as they've experienced it themselves.

Some of those people suffer breakdowns, depression, bipolar disorder, etc. and as those feelings of fear, anxiety, and anger grows, their depression becomes worse. Their whole personality changes and then don't even want to continue existing—because they don't like living in this world anymore. The term "burnout" is generally used to describe this situation, and many people in positions of responsibility have experienced it!

Their confidence in themselves to make sound decisions, and in people around them, becomes shaken. And their belief that God can get them out of this mess and all the negative feelings that have gripped them no longer exists. They can even blame God for letting this happen, and end up wishing they were no longer around to feel anyone else's pain. And yet even with that realization, their empathy doesn't shut off. And they think that the only way to protect them is to become extremely negative and stop caring for everyone or anyone.

They try and feel better by indulging in things that increase the dopamine levels in the brain, which is the feel-good chemical our brain naturally produces. But many, if not most of those activities that enhance the dopamine level, can be harmful, and all of them are short-lived, leading to addictions. Then those around them who were accustomed to dumping all their troubles on that person suddenly can't figure out why they're now so angry and aren't available anymore.

I've seen many meltdowns like this, and the road to recovery can take years, or decades, comes too late, or it never comes!

When a person loses confidence in themself—they can begin to doubt every decision they make, and also lose trust that they are hearing from God. They begin to think it is just their thought patterns that are involved in the decision-making process, and that's why it is all crumbling around them.

Physical illness can also cause a person to begin to lose confidence in themselves and others, as can the unexpected loss of loved ones. As an example, in the run-up to the year 2000, there was a lot of hype about the Y2K computer glitch that threatened to shut down computer systems all over the world. Having myself been advised of the potentially catastrophic consequences of this by programmers who write code, I too began to worry about its implications.

Now before you say that I and tens of millions of others just bought into a hoax, you need to talk to the computer programmers who worked non-stop re-writing code to avoid the worst of the problems, so it became nothing but a blip in history. One would think that the government and industry would not spend a lot of money on a hoax employing millions of programmers to work around the clock throughout the world, to fix a problem that they didn't think existed. But, when computer models produced the data to see the impact when the year 2000 ticked over, the result was catastrophic, which is why the USA spent $100 billion to de-bug their systems, roughly $9 billion by government and $91 billion by industry. Does that sound like it was a hoax? On top of that, the rest of the world spent between $300 and $500 billion to fix their systems.

You can read about it here if you're interested in finding out the truth:

https://slate.com/technology/2009/11/was-y2k-a-waste.html.

So why am I telling you this, you might wonder? It's because sometimes in life, even when we have useful information from the right sources and feel a need to act on them, the spirit can be telling us something opposite. This effect can happen in everyday life. It doesn't have to be something as widespread as Y2K was going to be. But—even though I knew it was going to be a problem and took steps to protect my family in the event of a grid shutdown, that inner voice was telling me not to worry; it will be okay. Every time I would spend money on something in preparation for this event, I'd get the same gentle urging not to worry, don't buy that, don't do that, it's not necessary, etc.

And after all the times in my life that I listened to *divine intervention* guiding me, proving that the advice was sound, did I listen to it this time—NO! Because I had experienced the "burnout," I have spoken of, and I didn't know what I could trust anymore. Why you might ask, was that the case? Probably two reasons would explain it. Part of it was ego, fully convinced that the Y2K bug was real. It was, of course, but it merely got mitigated with the work that $500 billion buys in less than two years to keep all systems operating. Yes, many small glitches took place in local areas, but no major cascading failures. Ego can keep you on a path that will lead to failure, even though that's not the direction or destiny you desire. But as the ego is a part of you, you hold onto it, hoping you are right so all your efforts can be justified.

You see this all the time when some group or denomination declares the time of the rapture, or the return of the mother ship to carry them away, or end of the world, etc. They hold onto their beliefs, despite the evidence to the contrary, because their self-worth is tied up in it coming to pass, and for them being able to say, "See, I told you so," is all that counts!

The second reason for me was that I had a feeling that the year 2000 was going to hold an event that would be devastating to my family or me, and I couldn't shake that feeling. So even though God or my guardian angel was telling me not to worry about preparing for Y2K, the sense of a looming traumatic event would not go away. And when January 1, 2000, came and went without a major glitch, but the feeling of something terrible happening stayed with me, I was disappointed that I had guessed wrong on Y2K, but concerned that the foreboding feeling persisted.

I had been taking care of my older sister, who was 44 at the time since her husband died suddenly, and they had cancelled his life insurance just a couple of weeks before because they couldn't pay the premiums. She had diabetes and was on peritoneal dialysis and stayed in the little house we had bought for her and moved out to our property.

In the spring of 2000, she decided to move to Edmonton to be closer to her doctor's appointments as the long trips were taking a toll on her. In late June, when I went to the city to take her shopping, she slipped off a curb while stand-ing near the front of my truck, waiting for me to get her walker. She severely broke her ankle, and because of diabetes and kidney failure, it would not heal. After almost two months of pain, they amputated her foot.

Then, in September, I got a phone call from her doctor while I was out hunting south of Rocky Mountain House, Alberta. I was told Don-na was in intensive care and that I should hurry. I prayed the whole way and drove from there to Highway 2 near Red Deer, Alberta, and up to Edmonton, covering just over 208 kilometres (130 miles) and sometimes doing over 160 kilo-metres per hour (100 mph) on the three-lane highway, for most of it, and never met a cop the whole time. I suspect that alone was a small as-pect of *divine intervention*.

My mom was there as well, as the doctor wanted to do exploratory surgery to see what the problem was, and we had to give our consent. I had to, that is. And then hours later, I had to con-sent to take her off life support as the surgery didn't go well. I lost the sister I loved after allow-ing them to do surgery, and they screwed up, then they willingly gave her an injection as we stood there, which ended her life in minutes. I guess that was my Y2K event, and since my older sister and I had gone through so much hardship in life together, it was tough to endure.

But then in the middle of the night in early November, just two months later, I got a phone call from B.C. My younger sister, Linda, who was only 30 years old, and had developed epilepsy after being on a diet program and taking certain medications, had died of a grand mal seizure. She had lain down on the couch to take a nap before dinner, which her husband was preparing, and her two little boys, roughly five and two years old, couldn't wake her. She was also eight months pregnant with her third child. So, my sense of foreboding about the year 2000 was real after all, just not in the way I anticipated it would happen.

I hate phone calls in the middle of the night, they always bring bad news, and I've had many of them over the years, including news about the death of my dad and mom.

Extremely emotional events can shake a person's confidence in their relationship with God, and then doubt easily creeps in as it gets a stranglehold on you. In 2006, I decided to sell our beautiful home in Alberta with a half mile of white sand beach and move us closer to our daughter and grandchildren in Saskatchewan for two reasons. My wife wanted to be closer to her new granddaughter and our daughter was constantly ill. She was on her second pacemaker, in a constant personality struggle with her in-laws, and wanting us to be closer. I had misgivings about it, but thought maybe it would work out.

They lived in a tiny old house in a little hamlet that was very hot in the summer and cold in the winter, and she was unhappy living there. We bought a quarter section of land with a house trailer and a large shop on it for them to live on, closer to his parents farming operation. And we rented a small very old farmhouse close by, in the hopes that we could build a place on their quarter section of land. We were hoping life would be better for them and also thought we'd have a place to retire to in later years. Unfortunately, things didn't work out as planned, and she, then divorced her husband in 2017 and took our three grandchildren to another province.

We felt abandoned, and very hurt to have given up so much to try and heal their relationship and seemed it was all for nothing in the end. In Jenny's attempt to start over, all ties were broken, denying us access to our grandchildren, even by phone.

We no longer had our beautiful home, nor my Super Stinson floatplane, jet boat or ATV's that I had worked so hard to purchase, and we were now renting an old farmhouse to be close to our grandchildren, and no longer had them either. Our investment in the farm and plans to build there were dependent upon their continuing relationship, so that was gone as well.

There's only so much the Spirit can do for you if you continue to ignore that gentle voice trying to get you back on the right track. As life around you, begins to deteriorate, all God can do is stand back and watch it unravel and be there to pick up the pieces, if and when, you come back around. Sometimes, you can love your children too much and sacrifice far too much for them, to try and give them a better life. When in fact, their life was better than yours ever was at that age. You may be willfully blind to it though, because your hope overrides the warnings you are given. Often, you only discover it when it is too late to salvage anything.

But it's not their fault! It's always a free will choice as love never forces its will upon you. If it did, then you would learn nothing and never appreciate the blessings of having something to enjoy, if you never experienced the loss of something you loved.

Somedays, it is easier to think that quitting this world would bring relief from the pain and betrayal one experiences. But then, the learning would stop as well, and we are here to experience and learn. There are some things in life, whereby, only God can bring any comfort and peace, if you will let him.

Is it *divine intervention* or just misfortune that some of us live to regret that old saying, *"You can pick your friends, but you can't pick your relatives."* Or is it that those difficult people in your life were exactly the ones you needed, in order to learn something, you wouldn't have without them?

The passing of both of my sisters was decades ago, and the ensuing loss of our hopes for the property, our grandchildren, and our finances, was just three short years. I am slowly coming around to realize that it's okay, but it still hurts from time to time.

Forgiving someone who has hurt you, and never asked to be forgiven, is not because they deserve it. It is because you deserve it, as it sets you free from the anger and resentment that traps you. It often takes a while though to let it all go, as it will keep coming back to claw at you, and you need to push it away to stay free from its strangle hold on your heart and mind.

With little savings, no assets, and no pension, we have no choice but to start over in our 60s, and pray that God will take care of us, as we try and be a blessing to others. Writing this book is part of that healing process, and I want to personally thank you for purchasing it.

I'm hoping that the richness of my life experiences, the good and the bad, will help you become prosperous in your relationship with God and with others on the same journey. Also that you will open your mind to the blessings that are available to you if you learn to trust that inner voice and recognize from where it comes.

# CHAPTER THIRTY-TWO

# Sanctuary

There were many other events in my life where God moved undeniably, and if you choose to read the other book titled: *'If Divine Intervention is Real, Do Hunters Experience It?'* you will learn about many more of them. But I would like to end this book with a story that took place in late 2008 and really what eventually led to me writing these books.

If you have read this far and are interested in my second book that focuses on *divine intervention* while engaged in outdoor activities like hunting, then you might be thinking that I've had everything work out wonderfully in life. You'd be wrong.

Many things in life can lead to events that take everything from you, and I've experienced many of them. Trying to help the family too much has depleted me financially, as I had a habit of giving away too much. Mainly because my father had not given me much, and I guess I overcompensated, as I didn't want to be like that. It ended up costing me my home and all my favourite possessions. In the end, it was not appreciated by those who received my generosity as I had anticipated they would.

Along with the loss of loved ones as all four of my family members had passed away by 2009, the ending of the inventory projects I had done so well on within B.C., my dear wife's battle with cancer, severe difficulties of my son's kidney failure, and family members in great legal difficulty. Added to that, the betrayal by people I trusted that ended up taking advantage of me.

So many things can cause a person to lose faith and trust that God will work something out for you. But it was never God's fault, it was always my decision, and I had received warnings to not proceed in some cases but ignored that *divine intervention.* It can be a long way back to what was before, but I'm taking that journey as you read this.

What a person holds onto is hope. Sometimes encouragement can seemingly come "out of the blue" as they say. It arrives in time to give you hope to make it just one more day. It would be easy to quit if you think there is no more hope, and that's why people do. But to find the strength "to cross one more river or climb one more mountain," it does take *hope*. It brings friends or loved ones to offer encouragement, or merely a stranger placed in your path at precisely the right moment. You may be that *stranger* for someone else if you allow God to use you for that purpose.

Those of you who have been there or are there now or recognize these feelings in people you care for will understand what I am saying. To those spared from this kind of *distress*, I encourage you to be that person who brings hope to someone who is going through various struggles that hit all at once, to break them down. I hope you can be that person who lifts them and encourages them to keep going.

At a particularly low time in my life after experiencing much loss and blaming myself—for many bad decisions, we found ourselves spending the winter months on Vancouver Island renting a home at Nanoose Bay. With my wife and youngest son, I hoped to have at least one warm winter in a warmer climate in my life. Even that wasn't to be; as in early November 2008, we had 47.5 centimetres (19 inches) of snow on the ground and sub-zero temperatures.

I should mention that my son and I are avid science fiction fans; Jeffrey has always wanted to be in a sci-fi TV series and had put quite a few quirky videos up on YouTube years ago. How this next event of *divine intervention* came about was the result of following the news about a new TV series called *Sanctuary*. An online post by an executive of the *Sanctuary* series stated that they were looking for writers for new episodes for their second season. I thought, well, why not send them some stories, and maybe they will give my son a chance to be in an episode in return. What I didn't know was that they had neglected to state that the writers must be part of the Writer's Union, or they couldn't even look at any submitted storylines.

Believing that we had a chance, I wrote two family-oriented episodes for *Sanctuary* and sent them off, although I had never written any screenplays before in my life. What I also didn't realize was that any unsolicited screenplays that came into their offices got tossed in the garbage. This process is standard practice in the industry to avoid any possible copyright litigation down the road.

I sent them off by the end of November with lots of hope, not realizing it was totally in vain. How would an outsider even have the proper connections? There is no way they ever allow an outsider in since it is an industry that is closed to anyone who is not well connected or part of the Union. On December 21, the day after Jeffrey's birthday, the phone rang, and the voice on the other end said it was Martin Wood, co-producer and director of *Sanctuary* and former director of *Stargate SG1* and *Stargate Atlantis* for nearly 15 years.

He said that by accident, my scripts ended up on his desk, and although they could not use them due to union regulations and legal implications, he appreciated me sending them to him. He then offered to give Jeffrey and me one day on set when *Sanctuary* started filming the first episode of season two. Having trouble speaking at that point, I handed the phone to Jeffrey, who talked with Martin for a short while.

It was a special gift to have received this opportunity being so near his birthday and Christmas; it felt surreal. Can you see how *divine intervention* had to take place for him to receive those unsolicited scripts that they are never supposed to open, let alone read them? And I know Martin had read them because he commented on them later on.

In the time between December 20, 2008, and January 31, 2009, I had a unique experience as I had a science fiction series unfolding in my mind when I would sleep at night, and I'd write down the episodes in the morning. Each morning I would begin to put the event down in print on my laptop and would stop after 25–30 pages, not because I was tired, but because the story shut off. I had no idea where the story was coming from or where it was going after that. Then the next morning, I'd wake up and continue to write another 25–30 pages to finish a one-hour episode. What was strange was that I could see it all unfolding in front of me like I was recording it, rather than making it up.

This process went on for 13 episodes in January, and I found it fascinating since I had never written any science fiction series before. I hadn't written much of anything, only two storylines for *Sanctuary*, and a couple of poems over the years. I didn't know the purpose of receiving this long science fiction series, as I already now knew that neither Martin nor any producer could accept storylines from me, because I wasn't part of the Writer's Union. And to become part of the Union, you would have had to have more than one script accepted by a producer and produced. But you couldn't get a producer to read one if you weren't part of the Union.

A real catch-22 scenario that guaranteed no one could bring new ideas to the industry unless you had exceptional connections, which I didn't. It's probably also why we see so many reboots of previous movies, TV series, or converting comic book stories into television shows and movies, instead of studios producing original content, because they are compelled only to use existing writers.

I had been fortunate enough to be accepted into the master's degree program at Royal Roads University in Environment and Management in January 2009 as I hoped it would help me get work again. I started the first-in-class sessions in February 2009, which ended at the end of March. We would then work on assignments until the next online session began in a couple of months before going back to the university again. My educational process went on until the spring of 2011; when I would hand in my completed thesis. So, I had something to occupy my mind while hoping that the offer from Martin Wood was still on the table.

Finally, near the end of March 2009, Martin called again, and the arrangements were made for us to attend a day on set. We were packed and stopped in Vancouver on our way back to the prairies to be ready for our day on set in Burnaby. Jeffrey and I spent the day as special guests of Martin Wood and Amanda Tapping. They toured us around the set and introduced us to everyone and had lunch with them at the catering trucks with all the actors and crew. They had our names printed on the sleeves that slipped over two director's chairs, which were placed beside Martin's chair as he directed scenes that day, and it was indeed a dream come true for us. But it wasn't over!

While Martin and Amanda were talking to us during the afternoon, they said they were already looking for their next production for when *Sanctuary* ended. It was like a little light turned on in my head, and I said that I had the whole first season of a family-oriented science fiction series, if they were interested. Martin said that I should send it to them and they'd take a look at it. Can you imagine the feeling that gave me after so many disappointments over the previous few years?

The next morning, after that beautiful experience, my wife, son, and I continued our journey homeward, with renewed hope for something great and exciting to take place in our lives.

That summer, I re-read the stories I had written and corrected some grammatical errors while also working on my master's degree. By September, we had sent the scripts off to Martin Wood, just before we returned to Surrey, B.C., for the winter, to be closer to my second intake at university. I hadn't heard from Martin for months, and I wondered what had happened to my storylines, and if he had a chance to read the pilot. It turns out, he hadn't had a chance to read them since they were so busy wrapping up their second season production, but finally, I got a reply from his secretary on January 26, 2010, saying that he'd get to them shortly.

On January 29, a Friday afternoon, Martin called me from his car during the rush hour drive home and said that the pilot was incredibly creative. They wanted me in their office the next Wednesday, February 3, 2010, to discuss acquiring it for their next production.

What he especially liked was that the technology used in the series was new and had never been featured in science fiction before and still hasn't, by the way. One particular piece of technology I dreamed up was a method of short-range subspace travel for the characters in the series and described how it was built and functioned. What was interesting to me was that six months later, my eldest son had found that very description of my imagined technology in an article on quantum mechanics theory, and it was called "Quantum Tunneling." And yet, I had never read anything about quantum mechanics at any point in my life. How's that for *divine intervention*? That phone call from Martin set my spirits soaring as I'm sure you can understand.

Jeffrey and I attended just after 1 p.m. on February 3, 2010, but as we entered their office, the atmosphere was different than before. It seemed tense and strained, and Martin took us into an office and closed the door. He proceeded to tell us that the creator of *Sanctuary* had his ideas for what their next production would be, and why should they consider anything from an unknown writer. I had heard before that it was an industry of egos, and had found out just how real that was. Martin apologized but said there was nothing more he could do for us.

It was crushing, of course, as so much hope was placed on that being what we would be doing next, but again, not destined to be the right time.

The series lay dormant until the late summer of 2019. I once again revived the idea that I could find a producer who might pitch the series to Netflix or Amazon or even a network that would produce a family-oriented science fiction series that the whole family could watch without their senses being insulted. I believe that one can enjoy inspiring drama, adventure, and conflict with the entire family, without being subjected to scenes not appropriate for younger viewers or sensitive spirits, if it's intelligent writing. I believe that the science fiction fans for *Star Wars*, *Star Trek*, and *Stargate* franchises, etc. are still out there and would like traditional family viewing adventures. I hope to offer it to a new generation of fans one day.

On contacting an actor in July 2019 from *Stargate SG1* about my sci-fi series, he directed me to his booking agent to have her read my scripts, and she told me she couldn't put them down. She then encouraged me to do an e-book and an audiobook of the series to gain public support, and then it would be easier to approach Netflix or Amazon, etc.

Because of this encouragement, I began converting my screenplay into a novel series to share with science-fiction readers. By the way, you can read the synopsis for the storylines of that Sci-fi series called *Earth Quadra* on our website earthquadra.com and judge for yourself if any *divine intervention* was in operation as I recorded the episodes each day back in 2009. I will eventually get the scripts all converted and make them available. I'm not the most colourful writer or the most articulate, but I believe that the series was inspired and did not come from my imagination alone. Perhaps one day, somebody who reads it will have the contacts, which will produce a family-friendly science fiction, space opera TV series, and bring these characters to life.

Shortly after that contact with the agent, my eldest son asked if I could write down some of the stories, I had told him while he was growing up so that he could pass them on to his children in the future. And this is how I started the book you have before you, '*Is Divine Intervention Real?*'

# Epilogue

I sincerely hope you have enjoyed these short stories and understand that every one of them comes from the memories I retained from real-life circumstances. A name might be missing here or there, or a date might be wrong, but the actual events occurred as described. I hope it has encouraged you to believe that God is working in your life as well, and the lives of your loved ones.

In the trying times that many of us live in currently, remember that *divine intervention* is just a thought away. The one, who provides it, never rejects an honest heart and only acts out of pure love and concern for your wellbeing. And if you mess up, quickly forgives and tries to make a way of escape for you, or attempts to put people or events in your path to heal your hurting soul.

I don't just believe there is a God or Universal Intelligence that watches over us and is there when we call—I know there is, because I've experienced it many times. Like calling 9-1-1, if you've never done it, you need to believe there will be a person there to answer because others have told you there is, and they have proved it to themselves. Is anyone skeptical of the claim that there are 9-1-1 operators available to answer your call? As long as they aren't already on the line helping someone else, of course, and you get a busy signal of a voice recording. The significant part is; you will never get a busy-signal from God. But if you have called 9-1-1 and someone answered, then you KNOW there is someone there ready to assist you. That's the difference between believing because someone else has told you, and knowing because you've experienced it yourself.

And of course, the only way to know for sure that there is a Divine Entity waiting to hear from you and be of help—is to make the call. But just like 9-1-1, they aren't there to provide three wishes for things that will make you wealthy or take advantage of others. They are there to provide help, guidance, and wisdom in a time of need.

There may have been days, weeks, months, or even years that have turned out badly in your life, and I can say that I genuinely know the feeling. But the best thing for you may have been the worst thing that ever happened to you, because it forces you to change your mind and see things differently. There is nothing more harmful or difficult to cure than a closed mind because it draws its strength from the ego.

God is always willing to save us in any crisis, but our ego often gets in the way, and we want to do it ourselves. Ego makes it challenging to admit that there is a much higher power than we are in this world, which is capable of love and compassion and the ability to help us do things that we could never accomplish on our own. That's why the ego fights against the acceptance that *divine intervention* is real.

In my opinion, having an inflated ego has never accomplished good things. I know it sure hasn't for me, and I have had lots of experience with it myself. It usually gets one into trouble with authority, destroys relationships, and discourages those around you from supporting you, because the ego is always toxic, even though the one with the puffed-up ego doesn't realize it.

For the skeptic, it might be easy to rationalize away some of my stories and justify in your mind that they were just a coincidence. But if even one of them cannot be explainable away as just pure luck, then you must concede that *divine intervention* is real. If you want an adventure in life, you should try and find out where it comes from, and who provides it. If you open your mind to the possibility, you will discover that the entity which offers *divine intervention* is always willing to work on our behalf the second we allow it and ask for the help we need.

The person who suggested this book to you would be an excellent place to start your journey into discovering a world that is vibrant and alive. It exists all around you, but your eyes may have been closed by choice, and has kept you blinded to its reality.

For the believer, the act of *divine intervention* is there to provide protection, guidance, hope, and to open doors of opportunity for you. It exists to help us grow in faith and trust. Throughout my life, I have been presented with opportunities that would make my life better, and it was always my choice to act on them or not. I have never received any large sum of money, which I haven't had to work hard for to obtain. When I was surrounded by doubt, I had neglected to act on opportunities that were presented to me on many occasions, only to regret it later when I realized I could have taken that path, and things would have turned out differently. But life is full of free will choices, and whether you make the right choice or not, *divine intervention* is always available to help you decide if you will trust it.

For believers, you already know the one who orchestrates it, and despite all your failings and restarts in life, it is always willing to begin again with a clean slate. It has never left you or ceased to talk to you and try to comfort and guide you. It may only seem that way because you have just stopped listening. I encourage you to continue your journey from where you left off, be sensitive to the spirit that wants to work on your behalf, so you can ask for help when you need it.

May God bless you, and I hope the other books in this series, which I believe have been inspired by *divine intervention*, will also bring you comfort and anticipation of what amazing things are available for you to experience in this adventure that God has set before us all.

Made in the USA
Columbia, SC
01 October 2020